BRILLIANT IDEAS TO GET BOYS WRITING

FOR AGES 7–9

Gillian Howell

First published 2009 by A&C Black Publishers Limited
36 Soho Square, London W1D 3QY
www.acblack.com

ISBN 978-1408-124-83-3

Series Editor Julia Stanton
Design © Anita Ruddell 2009
Cover photographs © Shutterstock
Illustrations © Bridget Mackeith

Photo credits: RS 6 Shutterstock/Andreas Gradin; RS 18 Shutterstock/javarman; RS 30 Shutterstock/Kimberly Palmer;
RS 33 Shutterstock/ bhowe; RS 34 Shutterstock/Ben Heys; RS 35 Shutterstock/Kirsz Marcinrs/Roberto Marinello; RS 50 Shutterstock/Chris Pole.

Printed in Great Britain by Martins the Printers, Berwick-Upon-Tweed

This book is produced using paper that is made from wood grown in
managed, sustainable forests. It is natural, renewable and recyclable.
The logging and manufacturing processes conform to the environmental
regulations of the country of origin.

**To see our full range of titles
visit www.acblack.com**

Contents

Introduction

Brilliant Ideas to Get Boys Writing aims to provide positive strategies and practical resources for boys, in particular, as they develop their writing skills in the classroom. All children become better writers by engaging in the process of writing often, although research in the last ten years has shown that boys face particular difficulties and therefore require targeted help to attain their potential. As in all learning, teachers are key to this process and many of the strategies to improve writing are the same for boys and girls, such as creating an inviting and creative environment. However, there are other strategies, such as an emphasis on 'active learning' and 'talk' which are more important to the acquisition of skills by boys.

The strategies which help boys become enthusiastic and independent authors, writing for different purposes and audiences are:

★ Creating an inviting environment
★ Providing good literature and text models
★ Planning for and understanding the writing process
★ Giving real and relevant reasons for (boys) writing
★ Creating active learning strategies, including talk and drama
★ The inclusion of visual media
★ The use of ICT
★ Planning meaningful cross-curricular activities
★ Using assessment and reflection

These strategies underpin all the activities and resources in this book. The activities are easy to follow and the instruction text has been kept to a minimum to make them less daunting for boys. All the activity and resource sheets can be used on their own or alongside other literacy schemes that are already established in your school. Throughout the book you will find lots of references to good literacy practices, such as shared reading and writing, adult scribing, demonstration, supported composition, in addition to the specific strategies to develop writing independence. Boys will develop and gain greater success and confidence in an atmosphere of support and encouragement. Praise from a caring adult can be the best reward for their efforts. The activities in this book will provide many opportunities for them to enjoy success and build confidence which, in turn, will develop a positive attitude towards writing and a resulting increase in self-esteem.

The writing process

The writing process is made up of specific steps. These are the steps used by all writers although, depending on the writing purpose and audience, some of them may be short-circuited. The units in Brilliant Ideas to Get Boys Writing develop these steps, giving emphasis to different features as the units progress.

The steps are:
★ **Pre-writing**
   Features talk and active learning strategies to gather thoughts and ideas, individually or in groups. Stage to define the purpose of the writing and the audience for the finished text.

★ **Making notes and drafting**
   Includes making notes of ideas and thoughts, discussing them and altering and adding to them. Stage to make first attempt at writing task and checking purpose and text type.

★ **Revising and polishing**
   The writer or writers improve their text, individually or in collaboration with others – altering and adding language features and improving vocabulary and text organisation.

★ **Editing and proofreading**
   Writers can check the language mechanics of their own text or have others do it for them.

★ **Reading and publishing**
   Sharing of text with audience, through a variety of media.

Brilliant strategies

Create an inviting environment

★ Have high expectations of boys
★ Engage and motivate reluctant boys
★ Promote confidence and creativity
★ Reflect boys' interests

Provide good literature and text models

★ Have available a varied mix of books which appeal to boys and reflect personal interests
★ Provide emotionally powerful texts and varied text types, including visual texts
★ Include literature with appropriate role models
★ Include popular and 'out of school' cultural models

Plan for and understanding the writing process

★ Plan brisk and structured lessons with clearly stated objectives
★ Include varied activities, building an understanding of the process
★ Demonstrate modelling of texts
★ Provide opportunities for paired and collaborative tasks
★ Use plenty of writing frames to provide structure, modify to suit tasks

Give real and relevant reasons for (boys) writing

★ Create a writing habit, a classroom focus, across subjects
★ Give choices in topic settings, particularly narrative
★ Use relevant topics and interests – boys respond well to real-world themes
★ Include an element of competition and allow boys to challenge themselves

Plan meaningful cross-curricular activities

★ Plan to introduce content and tasks from other subjects
★ Identify and use genres and text types associated with particular subjects
★ Plan writing tasks in specific subject areas to give boys a sense of real-world purpose

Create active learning strategies

★ Boys show a preference for active learning – provide opportunities throughout lessons
★ Use talk often – it helps boys in the formulation and articulation of ideas
★ Explicitly discuss models of writing and explore how writer's write
★ Use dramatic strategies, help develop understanding and expression

Include visual media

★ Boys respond to opportunities to work with visual media – cartoons, television, video etc.
★ Visual media as a starting point can help boys develop literacy and move to written text types
★ Use visual 'graphic organisers' to help structure text planning
★ Use visual texts to convey meaning and support written text types

Make use of ICT

★ Use multi-media text to stimulate discussion and ideas
★ ICT supports active and interactive task development and outcomes
★ Use ICT at all stages of the writing process
★ Use presentation software to increase boys' confidence

Use assessment and reflection

★ Set clear targets and link assessment to them
★ Give regular feedback, including individual progress
★ Use self-assessment and partner/peer review to encourage discussion of learning
★ Challenge boys to extend their writing

Worth reading

★ *Me Read? No Way!* A practical guide to improving boys' literacy skills – Ontario Education
★ *Improving boys' writing through visual literacy and drama* – Developed by Lancashire Literacy Team
★ *Literature search on improving boys' writing* – Caroline Daly, OFSTEAD

Using this book

For teachers:

Purpose, structure, language and visual features of text type.

Examples of 'forms' within the text type, or exemplars of the text type.

Suggestions for cross-curricular opportunities.

Notes for each activity, with emphasis on strategies to support boys' engagement and learning.

Challenges, opportunities, further activities to extend the unit.

Activity and talk-based ideas, which support boys learning, for getting started.

Links to numerous Resource Sheets and General Reference support materials available on the CD.

Suggestions for reflection and feedback opportunities.

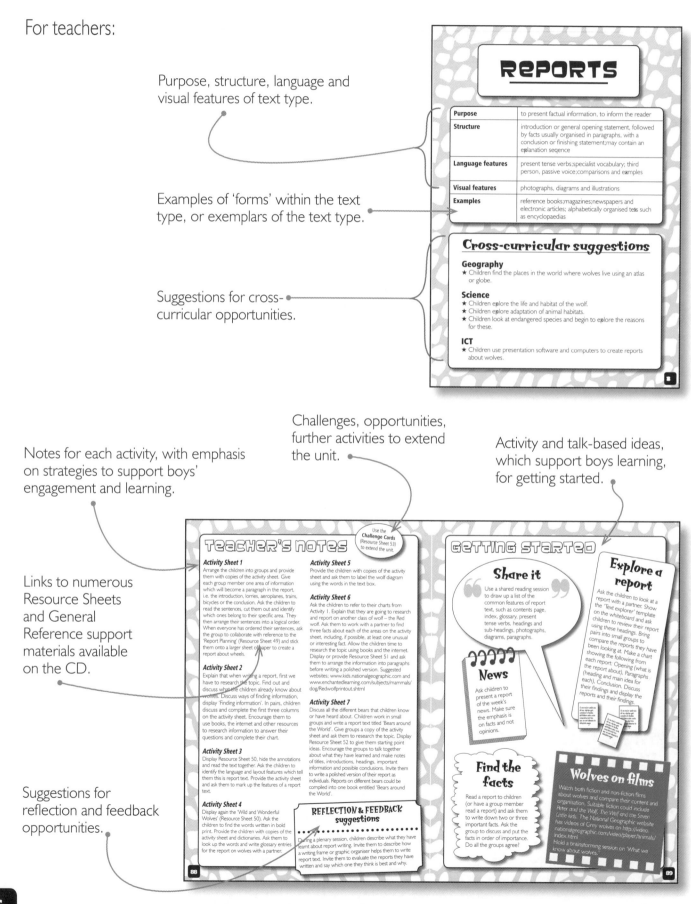

For pupils:

Activity Sheets
Up to nine Activity Sheets for each text type unit.

Learning Objective for each activity.

Emphasis on a range of strategies, exploring texts and building appropriate text type structure.

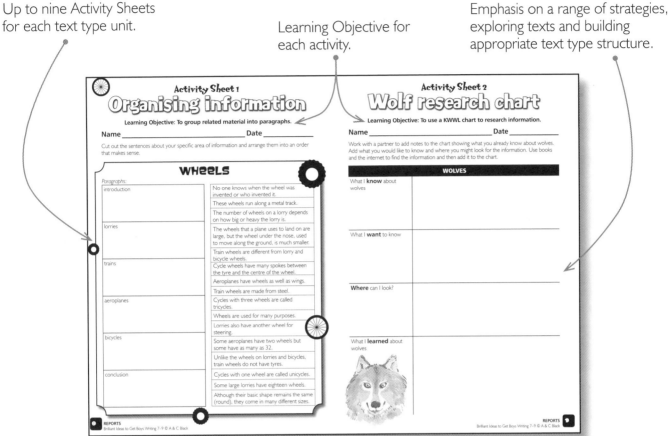

Resource Sheets
Resource Sheets to support and extend engagement with text type.

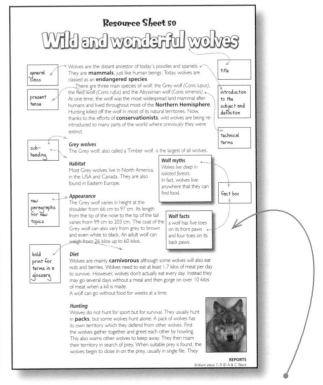

Writing frames to reinforce text structure in text planning.

Model text with structure and features highlighted, for display and discussion.

NARRATIVE FICTION

Narrative fiction is the telling (or narrating) of 'story' using many different forms. It includes the forms of traditional fiction, fold and fairy tales, fables, myths and legends as well as science fiction, fantasy, mystery and adventure, historical and contemporary fiction. Narrative fiction can be presented in many visual forms, including picture books and comic or cartoons.

★ Provide (and read) a range of appropriate texts as models, from genre being studied.

★ Share books which appeal to boys and provide opportunities to respond to them – role-play, dramatisation etc.

★ Provide electronic resources, if appropriate.

★ Create a bank of relevant vocabulary, phrases and prompts which help thinking, planning and reviewing.

★ Use *Talk for writing* principles and lots of opportunity to talk and collaborate prior to and throughout the writing process and dramatic strategies to promote high-quality thinking.

★ Display, demonstrate and discuss model texts and visuals and give a clear purpose for each task. Use genre terminology to ensure clear understanding of text structure and language features.

★ Ensure children discuss and agree text purpose and audience.

★ Provide questions which help the planning process.

★ Make available a range of tools, including ICT tools.

★ Display work in progress and finished work, in many different versions.

★ Ensure opportunites for review and reflection are available and provide effective feedback.

NARRATIVE FICTION

Purpose	to interest, entertain and amuse; sometimes also to inform and instruct
Structure	often sequential events; a clear beginning (introducing characters, setting & plot), middle (expanding on events and introducing the complication) and ending (resolution); sometimes includes flashbacks
Language features	usually past tense; mainly action verbs; descriptive language and dialogue; first and third person pronouns
Visual features	may contain illustrations
Examples	fantasy; realistic fiction; historical fiction; science fiction; mysteries; adventure; traditional fiction

Cross-curricular suggestions

Citizenship/PHSE
★ Encourage the children to discuss the story of 'The Boy Who Cried Wolf' and the implications or repercussions of playing tricks on other people.

Geography
★ Children can draw story maps or visual plans with labels to illustrate settings and events in the story.

ICT
★ Children can use ICT to write their story.

Teacher's Notes

Use the **Challenge Cards** (Resource Sheet 5) to extend the unit.

Activity Sheet 1

Read the model text together (Resource Sheets 1 and 2) using an enlarged copy or display them on an interactive whiteboard. Children work in pairs to identify the features of narrative writing. Discuss the layout, use of paragraphs and dialogue, verb tenses and punctuation. Ask the children what the dialogue adds to the piece, i.e. how would it be different if there was no dialogue? Children annotate the activity sheet (using the features listed at the bottom) to demonstrate the features of narrative writing and check their answers against the model text.

Activity Sheet 2

Read the model text again with the children before starting the activity. Discuss possible 'complications' for the plot. Children work with a partner and make notes on the sheet about the story so far and their ideas for continuing it on the sheet. Then enlarge a copy of Resource Sheet 3, cut out the paragraphs to make story cards and give them to children in groups. The children use the cards to create a sequential narrative by arranging them in order, discussing which belong to the beginning, the middle and the end. They can create a living story by holding the cards in story order.

Activity Sheet 3

Give the activity sheet to the children and ask them to make notes to describe each of the characters and the role they will play in the story. Children work in groups to role-play their ideas for their own story. They then use their notes based on their role-play and write a polished version of their story. The narrative writing frame (Resource Sheet 4) can be used to plan their story. Ask children to discuss their work with a partner.

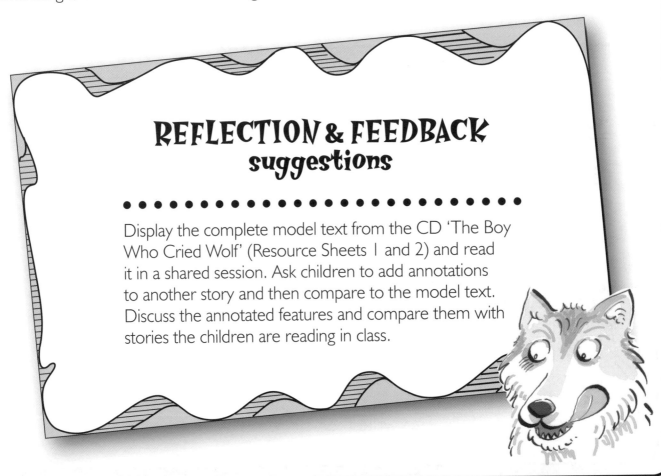

REFLECTION & FEEDBACK suggestions

Display the complete model text from the CD 'The Boy Who Cried Wolf' (Resource Sheets 1 and 2) and read it in a shared session. Ask children to add annotations to another story and then compare to the model text. Discuss the annotated features and compare them with stories the children are reading in class.

Getting Started

Display

Create a display of stories that appeal to boys. Enlist boys from the class to choose which books should be included in the display.

Characters

Ask children, in pairs, to decide on a favourite character and develop a short role-play. The rest of the class must guess who the character is. The role-play should provide clues to the character without mentioning his/her name.

Book group

Hold a group or class discussion about how the children choose books.

Ask what is the first thing you look at:
a) the title, b) the author's name, c) the cover illustration, d) the back cover blurb?

When you look inside the book do you:
a) read the first few lines,
b) look at the illustrations,
c) read the last page?

How important do you think the front cover or back cover blurb is?

Reviews

Create a wall display of book reviews written by children in the class and by other children in the school.

The story is really fantastic and so interesting. I couldn't wait to finish this book and find out what happened to all the characters.

What a boring book! Nothing happened. I could hardly make myself finish to end.

This is the best book I have ever read. I really liked the main character who is a boy just like me. He had lots of exciting adventures.

Re-tell

In groups of three, children re-tell some very familiar stories such as traditional tales. The first child tells the beginning, the second tells the middle and the third tells the ending. Swap parts around and re-tell another story.

Activity Sheet 1

The Boy Who Cried Wolf

Learning Objective: To identify the features that are common to fiction.

Name _____ **Date** _____

Jon was bored. The midday sun was beating down on the hillside where he sat in the shade of an old apple tree watching the goats. They were just mooching about grazing, or lying down. Nothing to do or see. It was dull and Jon was bored, bored, bored. He picked up pebbles as he sat and flicked them away from him one by one as he daydreamed.

"Nothing exciting ever happens," he said to himself. "If only I could stir up this dull old place..."

He stood up, stretched and gazed down on the village at the foot of the hill. The heat haze made it look even more sleepy than usual. Suddenly Jon had an idea.

"Those dull old people down there need stirring up," he thought. So Jon yelled at the top of his voice, "Wolf! Wolf! Wolf!"

Down in the village, the shopkeepers heard Jon's cry and hurried out of their shops onto the pavement.

"Quick!" cried Burt, the baker, and he grabbed a rolling pin. He ran up the hill as fast as his fat little legs could carry him, followed by all the other shopkeepers.

Down in the farms, the farmers heard Jon's cry too.

"Quick!" cried the farmers, and grabbing pitchforks and scythes, they ran up the hillside as fast as they could go.

When they arrived, red faced and sweating, they found Jon sitting in the shade.

"Where's the wolf?" they asked and Jon told them that it had run away when it heard them coming.

"Thank goodness for that," said the shopkeepers and farmers, mightily relieved, and they went back down to their shops and farms, talking as they went about how close Jon and the goats had come to great danger.

Jon laughed and laughed as he watched them go.

"Oh that was a laugh!" he chuckled, "I must do it again tomorrow. What a good trick!"

And so the following day, when Jon grew bored once more, he stood up and shouted at the top of his voice.

"Wolf! Wolf! Wolf!"

past tense verbs	time-based connectives	speech verbs	feelings	direct speech
reported speech	character descriptions	named characters	plot introduced
problem	paragraphs	setting description	story opening	main character introduced

Brilliant Ideas to Get Boys Writing 7–9 © A & C Black

Activity Sheet 2
Continue the story

Learning Objective: To make notes for a story showing beginning, middle and ending, plot, complication and resolution.

Name _____ **Date** _____

Make notes to help you continue the story.

How does the story begin?
Setting:
Characters:
What is the story plot?
Complication:
What happens next?
How does the story end?

Good words box

Activity Sheet 3
Characters

Learning Objective: To make notes about characters for a story, before writing a polished version.

Name _____ **Date** _____

Name and make notes about your ideas for each character in the story, their appearance and personality.

NARRATIVE FICTION
Brilliant Ideas to Get Boys Writing 7–9 © A & C Black

FAMILIAR SETTINGS

Purpose	to entertain and interest
Structure	often sequential events; contains a clear beginning, middle and ending; a problem and resolution; sometimes includes flashbacks; written in sections or chapters
Language features	usually past tense; mainly action verbs; contains descriptive language and dialogue
Visual features	may contain illustrations
Examples	*Matilda* by Roald Dahl; *Charm School* by Anne Fine; *Red Eyes at Night* by Michael Morpurgo

Cross-curricular suggestions

Citizenship/PHSE
★ Encourage the children to recognise and challenge stereotypical characters and behaviour in stories through role-playing alternative actions based on story events.

Geography
★ Children can draw story maps or visual plans with labels to illustrate settings and events in stories.

Art
★ Children can sketch and draw familiar settings, which they can use to illustrate their stories.

Teacher's notes

Use the **Challenge Cards** (Resource Sheet 11) to extend the unit.

Prior to the activities, read a story with a familiar setting or excerpts from a couple of stories with familiar settings and discuss with children why they are 'familiar'. Children could use Resource Sheet 6, 'Setting description' to summarise their discussions in small groups or with a partner.

Activity Sheet 1

Before the children begin the activity, display the image on Resource Sheet 6 and brainstorm what can be seen, heard, smelled and felt in this setting. Children work with a partner to generate ideas which they write on the activity sheet to describe the setting. When they have completed the activity sheet, encourage them to write a setting description to be used in a story about a football match.

Activity Sheet 2

This activity focuses on words that can be used to show the passing of time. Point out or highlight the phrase 'By the time' in the model text (Resource Sheet 7). Discuss how the use of time-based linking words can show the passing of time and the sequence of events in stories. Children write or draw three sequential events about a playtime on the activity sheet, cut them out and reorder them. The cut-out paragraphs can be swapped with three different children who read each one aloud or describe the drawing and decide on the best order to make sense of the sequence.

Activity Sheet 3

Discuss with children the difference between their day-to-day dialogue and 'story' or 'book' dialogue. Split the class into two groups to make a list of each set of words, then compare the lists.

This activity focuses on the role of dialogue in stories with familiar settings. Read the model text, (Resource Sheet 7) together using an enlarged copy or display it on an interactive whiteboard. Children work with a partner to identify the problem and predict how Bill will resolve it. Discuss the dialogue layout and punctuation. Ask the children what the dialogue adds to the piece, i.e. how would it be different if there was no dialogue? Children independently add the missing speech punctuation to the activity sheet. It might be useful to fill in and discuss the 'New words for old' sheet ' (Resource Sheet 8) prior to this activity to encourage them to think about the speech verbs used.

When the children have completed the activities, encourage them to plan and write a story based around a school football match. Suggest that they plan their story on Resource Sheet 9 or as a story map, draft their story, check and then write it. They should then share the story with a partner, make any final changes and publish it.

REFLECTION & FEEDBACK suggestions

During a plenary, encourage the children to talk about the role of dialogue in stories with familiar settings and its purpose and importance. In pairs, children mime the events from the model text and discuss how it changes without dialogue. Share and compare their football stories and encourage them to give feedback. What two things were well done and what one thing could be improved? Ask children to respond to a familiar settings story they have heard using Resource Sheet 10.

GETTING STARTED

Role-play

Pairs role-play a conversation that could continue the model text. Volunteers perform their role-play conversations for others and compare their ideas.

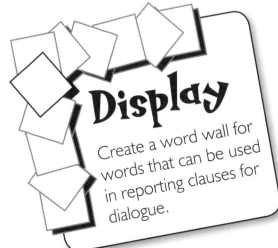

Freeze frame

Create freeze frame moments from stories being read. Invite the pupils in the freeze frame to describe a) what they can see, b) what they can hear, c) what they can feel, and d) what they can smell.

Display

Create a word wall for words that can be used in reporting clauses for dialogue.

?:/"*,\"!-.
Punctuate it

Create large punctuation cards for dialogue which include opening and closing speech marks, commas, full stops, exclamation marks and question marks. Distribute the punctuation marks among the children. Invite others to stand at the front and hold a conversation. The children with the cards have to hold up their punctuation mark beside each speaker before, during or after each child's spoken words. Alternatively, allocate different sounds to each punctuation mark using percussion instruments, hands or voices such as clap, click, whistle, stamp.

?:/"*,\"!-.

Blurbs

Provide several different stories with familiar settings. Children explore back cover blurbs and find similarities and differences in the settings and plots.

Setting description

Learning Objective: To describe a familiar setting.

Name _____ **Date** _____

How could you describe this setting? Add words and phrases that describe what you might see, hear, smell and feel in this setting.

See

Feel

Smell

Hear

FAMILIAR SETTINGS
Brilliant Ideas to Get Boys Writing 7–9 © A & C Black

Playtime paragraph order

Learning Objective: To write and sequence three paragraphs.

Name _____ Date _____

Use the word or phrase in the box to begin your paragraph.
Cut out the boxes and experiment with the best order.

All at once…

Suddenly…

At last…

Question mark, exclamation mark or comma?

Learning Objective: To identify the correct punctuation for concluding dialogue.

Name _____ **Date** _____

Choose the correct punctuation mark for these passages of dialogue and add Bill's reply to the end of the passage.

? ! ,

"Where do you think you are off to ⬜ "

"I am taking these books to the office ⬜ " replied Bill.

"Then get a move on ⬜ " snapped Lawrence, giving Bill a shove.

"Ouch ⬜ " yelped Bill. "What did you do that for?"

"Teacher's pet ⬜ " sneered Lawrence and shoved Bill again.

Suddenly a loud voice came from inside the office. "What is going on out there ⬜ " shouted Mr Davis. "Both of you in here at once ⬜ "

"I found Bill wandering the corridor looking shifty Sir ⬜ " said Lawrence before Bill could speak.

"Bill ⬜ " the headmaster asked.

_____

_____

_____

MYTHS AND LEGENDS

Purpose	to entertain; to convey a message or moral; to explain natural phenomena
Structure	sequential events; contains a clear beginning, middle and ending; a problem and resolution; lots of action and conflict; written in sections or chapters
Language features	past tense; descriptive language and dialogue; third person
Visual features	may contain illustrations
Examples	*Jason and the Argonauts*; *King Arthur and the Round Table*

Cross-curricular suggestions

History
★ Children can research figures from legends to explore whether they really existed or are fictional.

Geography
★ Children can draw story maps or visual plans with labels to illustrate settings and events in stories.
★ Children can find the places where myths and legends originated using atlases or globes.

Literacy
★ Children can record myths and legends for other classes to listen to. Encourage them to include sound effects.

Teacher's notes

Use the **Challenge Cards** (Resource Sheet 17) to extend the unit.

Activity Sheet 1

This activity focuses on inventing an animal character with supernatural abilities for a creation myth. Read together 'How the Land of the Midnight Sun came to be' (Resource Sheet 12). Explain that animal characters in creation myths often have human abilities, i.e. they can speak, and magical abilities. Invite the children to describe animal characters from other creation myths or to find them in the stories in the book display. Children work together in small groups to create a new animal character using the activity sheet. When they have each drawn their own version of the group's animal character, invite them to write a paragraph as a character sketch.

Activity Sheet 2

This activity focuses on planning a creation myth. Discuss any creation myths the children have read and what was created in them. Display Resource Sheet 13 and ask the children to make notes, using the model text as an example. Then ask the children to suggest ideas for a new creation myth, for example, the first sunrise/rainbow/trees and so on, using the activity sheet. They could use the character created in Activity 1 or a new animal if they prefer.

Activity Sheet 3

In this activity the children choose a hero and a villain and answer questions about each of them to create a 'Quest myth'. Discuss the common characters found in quest myths. Display Resource Sheet 14 and ask the children to say who they think the characters are (heroes or villains) and what sort of characters they might be (heroes on the top line, and villains below). They can choose a hero and a villain. Using the activity sheet, they read the questions and discuss their answers with a partner before answering the questions in writing. Ask them to add any 'Wow!' (especially good words) to the sheet.

Activity Sheet 4

This activity focuses on creating a story map for a quest myth. Display Resource Sheet 14, 'Perils of the quest' and discuss the places illustrated. Ask the children to add words to describe them, for example, the swamp: gloomy, slurpy, misty, murky and so on. Invite the children to describe the perils each place might hold for a hero. Provide the children with the activity sheet and ask them to give interesting names to the features and make notes of 'WOW!' words to describe them. Finally, ask them to mark the hero's journey on the map and to share their maps and describe what happens to the hero in each of the places. They can then begin to draft their story.

Activity Sheet 5

Display the legend text, on Resource Sheet 15 and read it together. Invite the children to identify the features of the legend and discuss how similar or different it is compared to the creation myth text. Ask them to fill in the annotation boxes on the activity sheet using the words in the box at the bottom of the page. Encourage them to add any other features they can think of.

When the children have completed the activities, encourage them to plan and write a myth or a legend they are familiar with using their own words or to innovate on a known myth using Resource Sheet 16.

REFLECTION & FEEDBACK suggestions

During a plenary, encourage the children to talk about the differences between creation myths, quest myths and legends. Invite them to say which they prefer and why. Discuss what makes a good hero in a myth or legend. Look together at their pictures of heroes and draw up a list of attributes needed for a hero. Repeat the activity with story villains. Encourage the children to write a complete character sketch for a hero or a villain and create a 'Heroes and Villains' display to accompany their drawings of heroes and villains.

GETTING STARTED

Story time

Read different examples of popular 'creation' myths and 'quest' myths to the children and explore their similarities and differences e.g. Greek quest myths such as *Jason and the Golden Fleece*, *Perseus and Medusa*; creation myths such as *How Men and Women were Made* by Margaret Mayo.

Heroes and villains

Ask the children to draw a hero and a villain from their favourite myth or legend, or from one of the stories in the book display. Create a 'Heroes and Villains' display.

The best

Ask children to choose their favourite myth or legend and display an image from each in the classroom or a school corridor. Ask others to 'vote' by adding a short comment to the image. At the end of a week count the 'votes'. If the voting is across the school, did the younger children 'vote' for a different tale? If so, discuss in class what this says about 'audience'.

Which myth?

Ask pairs of children to record a description of the main character from a myth or legend (or a setting) they are familiar with. Ask them to challenge another pair to guess the myth or legend after listening to the recording.

Interview

Put the names of characters from myths and legends into a hat. Children draw a name and then have to prepare to be interviewed as that character by a newspaper or television reporter.

Characters in creation myths

Learning Objective: To create an animal character for a creation myth.

Name _____ **Date** _____

Use the planner to write down the group's ideas for a new magical animal in a creation myth.
Fill in any other ideas in the last circle. Then draw your animal in the box.

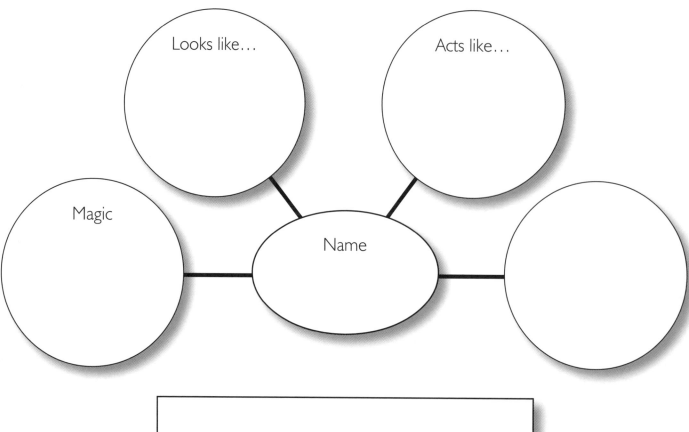

What, where, why, how?

Learning Objective: To plan a creation myth.

Name _____ **Date** _____

Make notes in the frame of your ideas for writing a creation myth.

How does the world look at the beginning of the myth?

What is to be created?

Are there people and animals in the world? Yes/No Write words to describe them.	**Where** are they?

Who creates it and how?

How does the world look at the end of the myth?

Heroes and villains

Learning Objective: To choose and plan characters for a quest myth.

Name _____ **Date** _____

Draw your chosen hero in one box and your villain in the other box. Answer the prompt questions about your hero and your villain. Add 'WOW!' words to help describe them.

How old is the hero?
Where does the hero live?
What is the hero's job?
Appearance
Hair...
Eyes...
Clothes...
Personality
Strengths...
Weaknesses...

My hero

My villain

What does the villain look like?
Why is the villain dangerous?
Personality…
Strengths…
Weaknesses…

Quest map

Learning Objective: To plan a journey for a quest myth.

Name _____ **Date** _____

Add words to describe each of the places on the map.
Draw your hero's journey through the island.

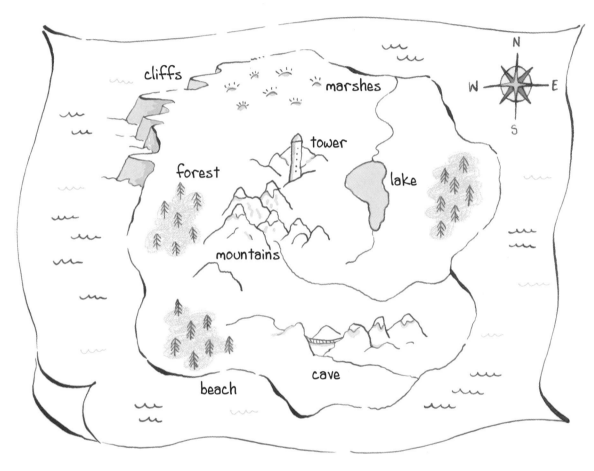

The journey starts…
Then…
And…
Finally…

How Arthur became King

Learning Objective: To identify the features of a legend.

Name _____ **Date** _____

Use the words in the box at the bottom to note the features of the legend in the boxes around the text.

Merlin had a problem. When the rightful King of England, Arthur, was born, Merlin had sent him to live with Sir Ector for safety until he was old enough to take the throne. But now the country was in a crisis. A new King was needed and many of the lords and knights were fighting over who should be king. Merlin knew that it should be Arthur if the people were ever to live in peace again, but Arthur was still only a boy. How could he convince everyone that Arthur was their true king?

A great tournament was to be held when all the knights in the land would attend, along with their stewards, servants and pages. Now Arthur was page to Sir Ector. He looked after Sir Ector's weapons and helped him dress before jousting, so this gave Merlin a bright idea. Somehow, he needed to show everyone how special Arthur was at the tournament.

Merlin sent out a proclamation. It announced that a sword had been plunged deep into a rock at the tournament. Whoever pulled the sword from the stone was the true king of England.

The knights were all very excited about this. They all thought they had a chance to become king and each one was sure he would easily pull out the sword.

On the day the tournament began, all the knights queued up to take a turn at pulling out the sword, even Sir Ector had a go. But not one of them, even the biggest and strongest knight of all, could move the sword a tiny bit. Not a centimetre. They were very puzzled, and of course, disappointed.

Sir Ector was in a bad mood after his failure to remove the sword from the stone, so when he returned to his tent and found that Arthur had forgotten to bring his tournament sword, he roared at him to go and fetch it at once!

Quickly Arthur ran through the town. He had to be fast as Sir Ector's first match would be starting very soon. But when he saw a sword sticking out of a rock at the edge of town, he stopped. 'I could just borrow that,' he thought. 'It'd be much quicker and I'll just put it back later.'

Arthur went over to the stone, grabbed the hilt and the sword slid smoothly out. He ran back to Sir Ector and handed him the sword.

"Where did you get this?" demanded Sir Ector.

After Arthur told him, Sir Ector marched Arthur back to the stone, followed by a great crowd of curious knights. He instructed Arthur to replace the sword and then tried to pull it out himself. The sword was stuck fast. All the knights tried again... and failed. At last Arthur walked to the stone and grasped the hilt. Once more, the sword slid smoothly out of the stone. Sir Ector gasped in amazement. He then went to Arthur, knelt before him for a moment and then, holding up Arthur's arm that held the sword, announced,

"Behold King Arthur, the true King of England."

| direct speech | reported speech | paragraphs | past tense verbs |
| words from the past | named characters | | |

ADVENTURE AND MYSTERY

Purpose	to entertain and intrigue
Structure	sequential events; clear opening, build up, plot, complication and resolution; often written in chapters or sections which may end in cliffhangers; author builds up tension and gives clues
Language features	past tense; descriptive language to create strong images; dialogue; written from first or third person viewpoint
Visual features	may include illustrations
Examples	*Cliffhanger* by Jacqueline Wilson; *Midnight for Charlie Bone* by Jenny Nimmo; *Flat Stanley* by Jeff Brown; *Ice Palace* by Robert Swindells

Cross-curricular suggestions

ICT
★ Children can create ICT presentations of their stories to include visual and audio material.

Literacy
★ Children can make word banks of 'adventure' and 'mystery' words. Remind them to include 'sound' words which could add to the atmosphere.

Drama
★ Children can create 'adventurous' situations, in groups and role-play them for the class. This may help others think of ideas for writing.

Teacher's notes

Use the **Challenge Cards** (Resource Sheet 23) to extend the unit.

Activity Sheet 1

Display Resource Sheet 18. Using a 'mysterious' or 'spooky' tone of voice, ask 'What could be on the other side of the door?' Discuss their suggestions. Give them the first few lines of an adventure or mystery story, such as: 'I heard the door creak. As I held my breath, it swung open. Should I go through it? Or should I run?' Ask them to write a paragraph to continue the story on the activity sheet.

Activity Sheet 2

Provide the children with the story openings on the activity sheet. Ask the children to read them and write whether they think they come from a mystery or an adventure story and to order them from the most to the least exciting. Then they choose the most exciting and write the middle of the story. Give them a finite number of minutes, about ten at most. Make sure they do not end the story – just write the middle. This is a useful way to stop children suddenly ending a story abruptly.

Activity Sheet 3

Display Resource Sheet 19 and discuss the characters' feelings. Ask the children to suggest a reason for the feelings and to say what the characters' next action might be. Explain how authors don't always tell readers exactly what is happening but give clues instead. This makes the reader feel more involved. For example, 'He opened his mouth in a silent scream,' tells readers that the character was terrified. Ask the children to complete the activity sheet with a partner and then share their paragraphs.

Activity Sheet 4

This activity focuses on making notes for a story to show a build up of tension or excitement. Invite the children to choose one story opening from Resource Sheet 20 or to agree one in their group. Ask them to use the activity sheet to make notes for the remainder of the story.

Activity Sheet 5

Discuss examples from stories where the author ends a chapter with a cliffhanger. Invite the children to say how this device makes them feel. Provide them with the activity sheet and ask them to finish the paragraph so that it makes the reader want to find out what happens next.

Activity Sheet 6

Provide small groups with the activity sheet. Ask the group to role-play the story from the prompts and add actions and events to flesh it out and make it more interesting. Ask a child to act as scribe for the group and write the story including all their role-play actions and events. Ask each group to read their version aloud and compare the similarities and differences.

Activity Sheet 7

Discuss the importance of including dialogue in adventure and mystery stories. Ask the children why it is useful to include dialogue, for example, to provide information about events in an adventure story or to allow characters to put questions into the reader's mind in a mystery. Dialogue should be included for a purpose, not just as everyday conversation, it must tell the reader something important. Too much dialogue can slow down the pace, but just enough can vary the pace so it is not all uninterrupted action. Children work with a partner to role-play the dialogue and then add the missing dialogue to the activity sheet.

REFLECTION & FEEDBACK suggestions

Display Resource Sheets 21 and 22 for the children to use to review adventure and mystery titles from the library. Can they identify each of the elements in each story? Suggest that they refer to these resources when writing their own adventure and mystery stories.

GETTING STARTED

Book display

Make a book display of adventure and mystery stories chosen by the children. Discuss what makes adventure and mystery stories different from other fiction genres. Draw up a class list of their ideas.

Props

Provide the children with artefacts or pictures that could feature in adventure or mystery stories, such as a key, a bag of coins, a 'wanted' poster, a scarf, or a spade. Invite them to choose an artefact and suggest what part it could play in an adventure or a mystery.

Adventure path

Display the 'Adventure Path' or the 'Mystery Tour' (Resource Sheets 21 and 22). Using an adventure story the class is reading or is familiar with, compare how that story follows the 'Adventure Path'.

Which character?

Play an 'adventure character' name game. Write some stereotypical detective names or adventure hero names on slips of paper and put them in a bag. Ask the children to pull one name out of the bag and draw a picture of a character to fit the name. When they have all finished, write the character names on the board. The children hold up the pictures one at a time and the others guess the character name that fits the picture.

What happened?

Ask the children to write down a title for an adventure story on a slip of paper. It could be one they have read or an invented one. Arrange them into small teams. Swap the team's story titles with different teams. Each team member reads the title on their slip of paper and says what they think might happen in the story. If they are close to the original title-writer's idea they get a point. The team with the most points wins.

Activity Sheet 1
The other side of the door

Learning Objective: To continue a story.

Name _____ **Date** _____

Write a paragraph about what is on the other side of the door and what happens to you.

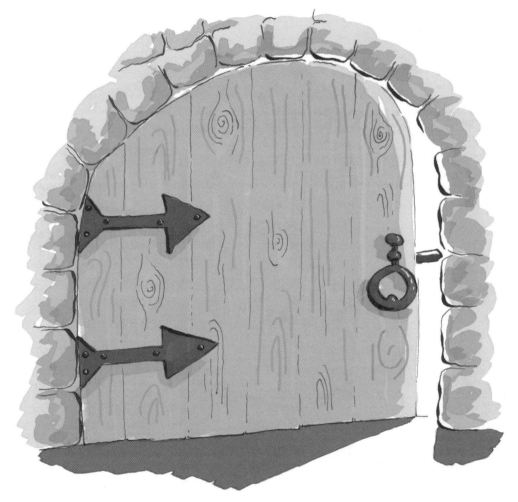

I heard the door creak. As I held my breath in anticipation, it swung open a fraction. Should I go through it? Or should I run?

_____

_____

_____

_____

_____

ADVENTURE AND MYSTERY
Brilliant Ideas to Get Boys Writing 7–9 © A & C Black

Story openings

Learning Objective: To understand the importance of grabbing the readers' attention.

Name _____ **Date** _____

What sort of stories are these? You can use the list of genres at the bottom to help you. Which are the most exciting?

Long ago, there was a boy who lived alone in a forest. He didn't know why he was alone. He just was. Always had been. And he thought he always would be, until they came…	
Donny Mack always walked home from school the same way. Down the road, along the tow path and then over the bridge. It was the quickest way home. So on Friday he went down the road, along the tow path... and along...and along. He stood, scratched his head and looked back along the canal. He looked up the canal. No bridge! No sign there ever was one!	
The Joneses lived in a semi-detached house in an estate of semi-detached houses. Each house looked almost the same. The only differences were the colour of the paint on the doors and windows. Theirs were painted pale blue. Mr and Mrs Jones went off to work at the same time every morning. Jonny and Janie Jones went off to school at the same time. Nothing ever changed.	
"You keep away from me and my dog!" The voice came from the other side of a high stone wall. "You hear me? Just keep away!" There was something about the voice that made me feel uneasy. I couldn't quite put my finger on it, but it was sort of angry, sort of panicky, sort of, well, terrified I suppose. I was desperate to see what was going on, but the wall was too high to see over. I was supposed to be going to the shop for Mum but instead I ran along the wall looking for an opening.	
Jacob did not want to go to summer school. Most definitely, absolutely, set-in-stone not! "You'll enjoy it, you know you will," argued his mother, but Jacob knew it would be full of geeks and shadows and he would be classed as the same. As usual, his mother won and so Jacob set off gloomily on Monday morning.	

mystery	adventure	familiar settings	traditional story

How do they feel?
What do they do?

Learning Objective: To give clues about characters' feelings and actions.

Name _____ **Date** _____

Write a paragraph to convey the emotion in each picture, without saying what the emotion is. Include what the character will do next.

ADVENTURE AND MYSTERY
Brilliant Ideas to Get Boys Writing 7–9 © A & C Black

Build up excitement

Learning Objective: To plan a story showing a build up of excitement or tension.

Name _____ Date _____

Make notes to build up the excitement in your story. Start at the bottom!

complication...

problem...

resolution...

first event...

opening...

ending

Cliffhanger

Learning Objective: To end a paragraph so that readers want to find out what happens next.

Name _____ **Date** _____

Continue the middle part of this story so that readers really want to start the next chapter!

Donny's breath came in short gasps and his chest heaved with effort as he scrambled on to the top of the wall. At first he could see nothing so he slumped on the rough stones, disappointment welling up in his eyes.

_____

_____

_____

_____

_____

_____

_____

_____

_____

Flesh out the story

Learning Objective: To use role-play as a device for improving a story outline.

Name _____ **Date** _____

1 Three children find a box on a beach. They open the box and find it is full of gold.

2 Two men appear and shout at them. The children run along the beach and hide in a small cave.

3 The tide comes in and they are trapped. Above, the men stand on the cliff top and begin climbing down.

4 A lifeboat arrives and rescues the children. The men are arrested for theft.

5 The children get a reward for recovering the stolen gold.

Dialogue

Learning Objective: To give readers information about events through dialogue.

Name _____ **Date** _____

What would you say? Add missing dialogue to the paragraph of this mystery story.

Owen carefully followed the trail as it led up to the door.

" _____ ", he whispered. Jack turned and

went back to the window. He looked out onto the street, but as Owen turned the key,

he couldn't help but want to see what was in the room too.

" _____ ", he said.

Suddenly, they heard a dreaded sound. " _____ ",
gasped Jack.

The boys quickly opened the door, dashed into the room and shut it behind them.

" _____ ", whispered Owen.

They sat for some time, breathing heavily, not daring to say a word.

" _____ ", squeaked Jack.

" _____ ", murmured Owen.

HISTORICAL SETTINGS

Purpose	to entertain and sometimes to inform
Structure	usually sequential; beginning, middle and ending; written in chapters or sections; sometimes includes flashbacks
Language features	past tense verbs; vocabulary relevant to the historical period and authentic detail; descriptive language and dialogue
Visual features	may include illustrations
Examples	*Friend or Foe* by Michael Morpurgo; *Smith* by Leon Garfield

Cross-curricular suggestions

History
★ Children explore how children's lives were similar and different in past times.
★ Children make a list of buildings and places associated with periods of history, then add words to describe them.

Drama
★ Children cut out pictures of people from other times and put them in a hat. They draw them out one by one and describe them to the group to see if they can guess who the character is.

ICT
★ Children can create ICT presentations of their stories to include visual and audio material.

Teacher's notes

Use the **Challenge Cards** (Resource Sheet 28) to extend the unit.

Activity Sheet 1

Children work with a partner on Resource Sheet 24, and decide if the words and phrases are from the past or the present. When they have finished, ask them to cut out the words and together, arrange them into a timeline order, beginning with the furthest back in history up to the present day. With the class explore the 'Tudor ships' (Resource Sheet 25) and discuss the setting. Give children the activity sheet and ask them to write what they can see, hear, feel and smell. You could play Tudor music while children are completing the work.

Activity Sheet 2

Using the activity sheet, or the 'Viking village' (Resource Sheet 26), children 'explore' the Viking village. They write what they can see, hear, feel and smell on their activity sheet. When both Tudor and Viking activities are completed hold a discussion about the similarities and differences in the settings. Invite them to describe what they would **not** see, hear, feel and smell in these settings.

Activity Sheet 3

Using the activity sheet, the children explore a setting where children are being evacuated in World War 2. Ask them to imagine they are one of the children in the picture. Where are they? Ask them to write what they see, hear and smell, then to write a paragraph that describes the emotions of the children in the setting. It might be useful to brainstorm ideas before writing using 'Evacuation spidergram' (Resource Sheet 27).

Activity Sheet 4

In this activity, the children make notes for a character sketch for a boy being evacuated in World War 2. When they have completed the activity sheet, encourage them to write a short character sketch to describe the boy in the drawing.

Activity Sheet 5

In this activity, the children use the character they described in Activity sheet 4 but place him in another setting and write a paragraph using words that show the passing of time.

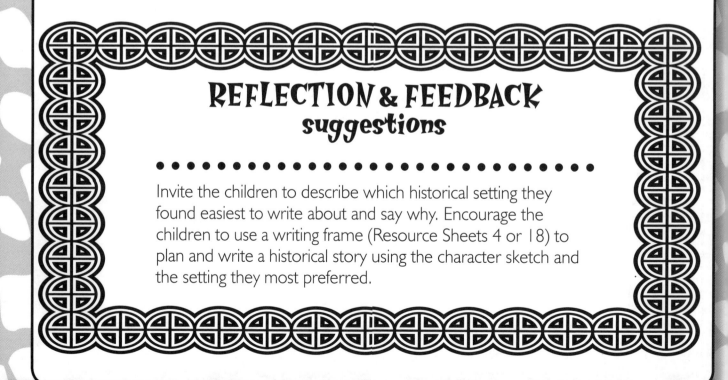

REFLECTION & FEEDBACK suggestions

Invite the children to describe which historical setting they found easiest to write about and say why. Encourage the children to use a writing frame (Resource Sheets 4 or 18) to plan and write a historical story using the character sketch and the setting they most preferred.

Getting Started

Not in use

Create a word wall of vocabulary that has fallen out of use, collected from reading the historical stories.

History stories

Read short stories with historical settings to the children, for example, *Flying bombs* by Dennis Hamley, *The Prisoner* by Penny McKinlay, (set in World War 2), *Penny Post Boy* by Karen Wallace, *The Sewer Sleuth* by Julia Jarman, (set in Victorian times), and *London's Burning* by Karen Wallace or *Viking Raiders* by Karen Wallace set in pre-Tudor times.

Old clothes

Provide the children with historical costume illustrations and invite them to label the pictures with the correct period.

Evacuees

In small groups, role-play a scene about children being evacuated in World War 2, or make it into a radio play. Explain that the children are on a railway platform waiting for a steam train to take them to the safety of the countryside without their parents.

Historical language

Arrange children into pairs. Using the period from a story being read, encourage the children to role-play conversations using the language and vocabulary of the period.

Tudor ships

Learning Objective: To generate vocabulary to describe a historical setting.

Name _____ **Date** _____

Imagine you are in a Tudor battle.
What can you see?
What can you smell?
What can you hear?
What can you feel?

see

smell

hear

feel

Write your description.

_____

_____

_____

_____

_____

_____

HISTORICAL SETTINGS
Brilliant Ideas to Get Boys Writing 7–9 © A & C Black

Activity Sheet 2
Viking village

Learning Objective: To generate vocabulary to describe a historical setting.

Name _____ **Date** _____

Imagine you are in a Viking village. What can you see? What can you smell? What can you hear? What can you feel?

see

smell

feel

hear

Write your description.

_____

_____

_____

_____

_____

_____

Evacuation!

Learning Objective: To describe a setting and empathise with a character.

Name _____ Date _____

Imagine you are one of the children in the picture. Write a paragraph to describe what you can see, hear and smell. Then describe how you are feeling about being evacuated.

_____

_____

_____

_____

_____

_____

Character sketch I

Learning Objective: To plan vocabulary for a character sketch.

Name _____ **Date** _____

Make notes to help you describe your character.

Who is this boy?

What does he
look like?

What is he
like?

Where is he
going?

What does he
feel about it?

Good Word Box

Character sketch 2

Learning Objective: To use vocabulary appropriate for a different historical setting.

Name _____ **Date** _____

Write a paragraph about your character from Activity Sheet 4, where does he go? What does he do? Don't forget to use the senses of sight, sound, smell and feelings! Use words to show the passing of time. There are examples to help you in the word box.

Word box
When, Later, Suddenly, All at once, While, After a moment, At last

IMAGINARY WORLDS

Purpose	to entertain and interest
Structure	usually written sequentially; clear beginning, middle and ending, plot, problem, complication, resolution; written in chapters or sections
Language features	past tense verbs; action verbs; descriptive language to create vivid images; dialogue; first and third person pronouns
Visual features	may contain illustrations
Examples	*Ice Palace* by Robert Swindells; *Planet of the Robots* by David Orme

Cross-curricular suggestions

ICT
★ Children use photo-processing software to create an annotated image of an imaginary setting for a story. Children could swap settings with a writing partner.

Art
★ Children draw and paint imaginary characters, and sculpt props for the imaginary world.

Geography
★ Children can draw story maps or visual plans with labels to illustrate settings and events in stories.

Teacher's notes

Use the **Challenge Cards** (Resource Sheet 32) to extend the unit.

Activity Sheet 1

In this activity the children rehearse telling a story using pictures as a stimulus. Display an enlarged copy of the activity sheet and model telling the story. Give the activity sheet to children and ask them to tell the story to a partner. Children could record their stories and play them back for classmates later.

Activity Sheet 2

Display an enlarged copy of the activity sheet. Discuss the illustrations, encouraging the children to use their senses to describe what is happening. The children write a paragraph for each picture to tell the story on their activity sheet. They then draw and write the ending. After the activity, check which (if any) connectives children used. Cut out the connectives cards on Resource Sheet 29 and place them face down on a table. Arrange the children into small groups. Give the children an opening sentence for a story set in an imaginary world, for example 'In the town of Wargle there lived a boy called Dax'. Ask them to continue the story, going around the group by adding two sentences each. Explain that they must pick up a connective card and use it to begin their second sentence. You can simplify the activity by grouping the cards so the temporal connectives, causal connectives and adverbial connectives are in separate piles.

Activity Sheet 3

This activity focuses on choosing adjectives to describe the atmosphere of the setting in an imaginary world. Show the 'Atmosphere' image from Resource Sheet 30 to the class, discuss and add appropriate words. Then ask children to complete the activity with a writing partner.

Activity Sheet 4

In this activity, the children place themselves into an imaginary setting and continue the story. Before beginning the activity, hold a shared writing session to gather ideas about using the senses to describe a new setting e.g. an alien planet, a deserted castle or your home in a time long ago.

Activity Sheet 5

In this activity, children use a story planner map to gather ideas for a story in an imaginary world. When they have added their ideas to the map, invite them to draft and write the story.

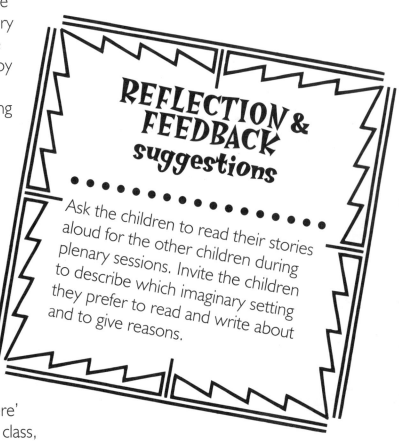

REFLECTION & FEEDBACK suggestions

Ask the children to read their stories aloud for the other children during plenary sessions. Invite the children to describe which imaginary setting they prefer to read and write about and to give reasons.

Getting Started

Story display

Invite the children to create a display of stories set in imaginary worlds.

Discuss settings that feature in stories in imaginary worlds. Create a list of settings and their features from stories the children have read and add other settings from their suggestions.

Hot seat

Invite the children to choose a character from a story set in an imaginary world. Ask them to sit in the 'hot seat' in the role of their chosen character. Ask the other children to ask the character questions about the imaginary world.

Shared world

Choose an imaginary world on which to focus. Create a class picture of the imaginary world and invite the children to add features from their own drawings. Ask them to write good words and phrases to describe the features of this imaginary world.

Compare

Play a DVD of a story set in an imaginary world to the children, for example, The Lion, the Witch and the Wardrobe, or The Wizard of Oz. Ask children to compare the DVD to the novel using Resource Sheet 31.

Imaginary characters

Discuss imaginary characters from stories set in imaginary worlds. Encourage the children to invent characters of their own and to draw and label the characters.

Telling a story

Learning Objective: To tell a story based on a sequence of illustrations.

Name _____ **Date** _____

Look carefully at each of the pictures. Tell your partner a story that includes each picture.

Brilliant Ideas to Get Boys Writing 7–9 © A & C Black

How does the story end?

Learning Objective: To write a paragraph for two illustrations and draw and write an ending.

Name _____ **Date** _____

Write a paragraph for each picture to tell the story. Draw and write your own ending.

1
_____
_____
_____
_____
_____
_____
_____

2
_____
_____
_____
_____
_____
_____
_____

3
_____
_____
_____
_____
_____
_____
_____

Atmosphere

Learning Objective: To choose words that are appropriate for describing the atmosphere of a setting.

Name _____ Date _____

Choose the four best words from the box below to describe the atmosphere. Add two more of your own.

Word box

bleak, bright, warm, dark, fearful, light,
gentle, harsh, soft, gloomy, grey

IMAGINARY WORLDS
Brilliant Ideas to Get Boys Writing 7–9 © A & C Black

What happens next?

Learning Objective: To continue a story in an imaginary world using the first person.

Name _____ **Date** _____

Imagine you wake up one morning and your bedroom has vanished. You are in a strange world. Read the opening of the story and write about what is different.

When I woke up that morning, I felt quite strange. My bed felt odd. Something was wrong. Instead of smooth white sheets and my comfy warm duvet, I felt …

_____

_____

_____

_____

_____

_____

_____

_____

Activity Sheet 5
Story planner

Learning Objective: To write notes of ideas for a story.

Name _____ **Date** _____

Make notes of ideas for your story using the story map. Write your ideas inside the circles. Add extra lines and circles of your own.

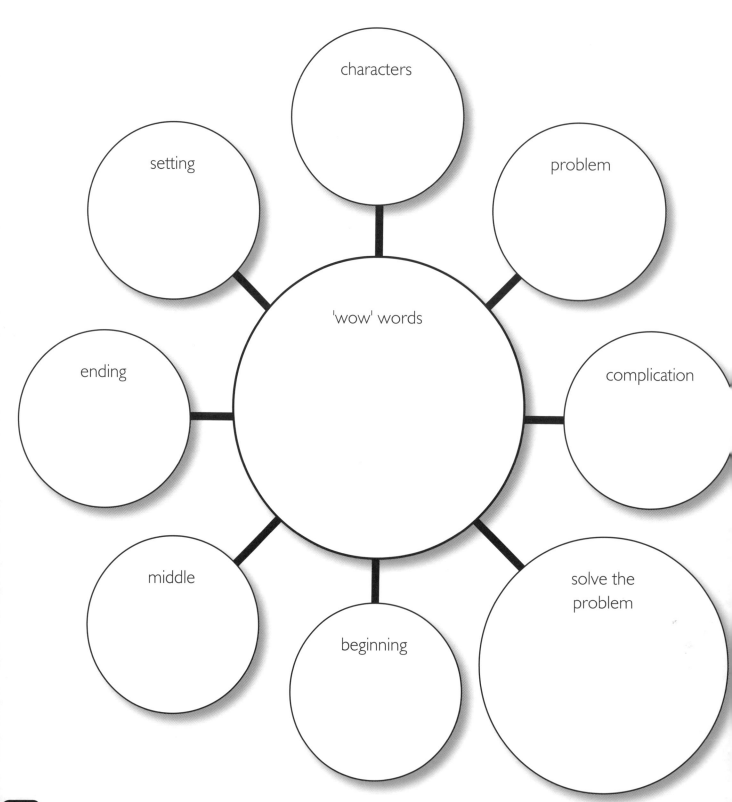

STORIES FROM OTHER CULTURES

Purpose	to entertain and inform about other cultures
Structure	sequential events; a clear beginning, middle and ending; often in chapters or sections
Language features	usually past tense; descriptive language creates images and authentic details; first or third person
Visual features	may contain illustrations
Examples	*Gregory Cool* by Caroline Binch; *Bamba Beach* by Pratima Mitchell

Cross-curricular suggestions

Geography
★ Children find the places where the stories originate or are set using an atlas or globe.

PHSE/Citizenship
★ Children explore the culture and way of life in different parts of the world.

ICT
★ Children can create ICT presentations of their stories to include visual and audio material.

Teacher's notes

Use the **Challenge Cards** (Resource Sheet 36) to extend the unit.

Activity Sheet 1

Display a copy of one of the rainforest images, Resource Sheets 33 and 34. In pairs, the children draw up a list of vocabulary that could be useful for a story in the setting. Draw their attention to the different groups of people – locals and travellers. Then display an enlarged copy of the activity sheet. Discuss the illustration, encouraging the children to use their senses to describe what they can see, hear, smell and taste. Give the children the activity sheet and ask them to write their descriptive words on it and to write a paragraph using the senses words to describe the setting.

Activity Sheet 2

In this activity, the children invent a character for a story set in a rainforest and for a story set in an African market. Display Resource Sheet 35 on the whiteboard and discuss the setting and how it might influence the people who live there. Children then draw what the character looks like and wears on their activity sheet and choose adjectives to describe their characters' personalities.

REFLECTION & FEEDBACK suggestions

Ask the children to read their stories aloud for the other children during plenary sessions. Invite the children to describe which setting they would prefer to read and write about and to give reasons. Discuss how the setting affects the plot and character in stories from other cultures.

Activity Sheet 3

In this activity, the children research and list words that could be used to create the settings for each of the three different scenarios from other cultures suggested on the activity sheet. They then plan a story from one of the three cultures. When they have added their words and their ideas to the story map, invite them to write the story. (The story frame on Resource Sheet 4 could be used to plan the whole story, prior to drafting and writing.)

Getting Started

Favourite character

Choose a character from one of the stories from other cultures you have recently read. Ask the children to discuss the character with a partner. Use a shared writing session to generate words to describe the character.

Freeze frame

Invite small groups to freeze frame a moment from one of the stories from other cultures they are reading. Ask them to say what they can see, hear, and smell at that moment. Invite them to describe what they are thinking.

Comparing cultures

Read several short stories from other cultures and compare similarities and differences. Using one story, ask the children to note what is different about the culture in the story from their own culture.

Hot seat

'Hot seat' children in the role of a character from a story from other cultures. Invite the other children to ask questions about the culture and how it differs from their own.

Book display

Encourage the children to create their own book display of stories from other cultures that they have enjoyed or think they might enjoy.

Activity Sheet 1
African market

Learning Objective: To generate vocabulary using the senses to describe a setting.

Name _____ **Date** _____

Imagine you are in this setting. What can you see, hear, smell, taste and feel?

see

hear

smell

feel

taste

STORIES FROM OTHER CULTURES

Characters in other cultures

Learning Objective: To create a graphic character sketch.

Name _____ **Date** _____

Draw a character from another culture and describe your character.

Lives

Enjoys

Behaves

Hates

Personality

1. What sort of hair have they got?
2. What clothes do they wear?
3. How do they move about?
4. How do they behave?
5. What do you think they enjoy doing?
6. What do you think they hate doing?
7. What words describe their personalities?

Activity Sheet 3
Three stories

Learning Objective: To sort vocabulary into appropriate groups for stories from different cultures and use it to tell a story.

Name _____ Date _____

Choose one of these three different settings: rainforest, African market or Australian outback. With a partner make a list of words which would be appropriate to a story in one of the cultures and put them in the box at the bottom of the page.

Now make notes of ideas for your story using the story map. Write your ideas inside the circles. Add extra lines and circles of your own.

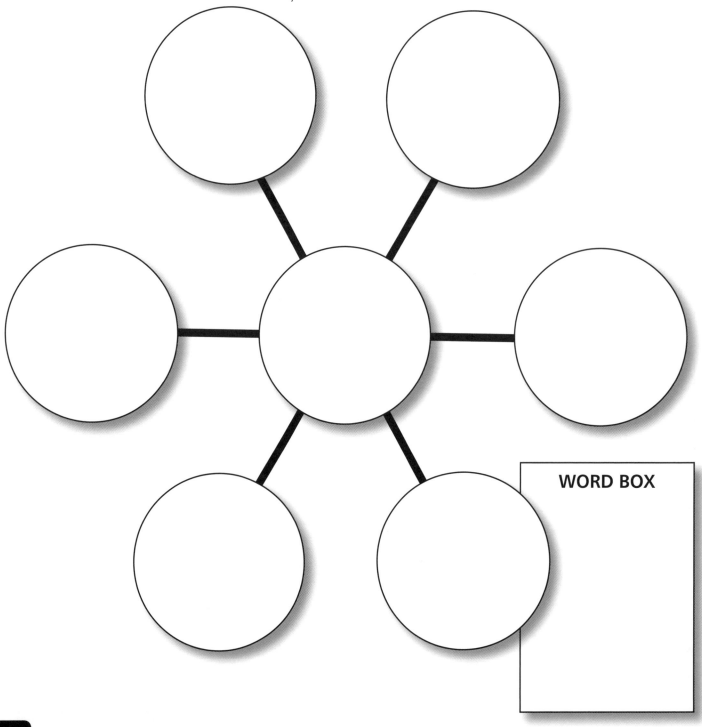

WORD BOX

STORIES FROM OTHER CULTURES
Brilliant Ideas to Get Boys Writing 7–9 © A & C Black

ISSUES AND DILEMMAS

Purpose	to entertain and to explore and resolve relevant issues
Structure	sequential order; strong plot; clear problems and resolutions; often in chapters or sections
Language features	usually past tense; descriptive language; strong adjectives to describe characters and setting; first or third person
Visual features	may contain illustrations
Examples	*The Fib and Other Stories* by George Layton; *The Angel of Nitshill Road* and *Bill's New Frock* by Anne Fine; *How to Live Forever* by Colin Thompson; *Underground to Canada* by Barbara Smucker

Cross-curricular suggestions

PHSE/Citizenship
★ Children explore how to deal with problems and discuss those people who could help (parents, teachers, siblings, peers, other responsible adults, school council etc.). Use role-play and hot seating to allow children time to explore these issues.

History
★ Ask children to think about the issues children in another time might have had. Are they the same or different to the ones they meet in their lives?

ICT
★ Children can create ICT presentations of their stories to include visual and audio material.

Teacher's notes

Use the **Challenge Cards** (Resource Sheet 38) to extend the unit.

Activity Sheet 1

Display an enlarged copy of the activity sheet. Use a shared writing session to explore the dilemma. Should Jon give the purse to the lady or should he keep it? What might happen to the lady and to Jon if he takes either course of action? Ask the children to work with a partner and create two alternative courses of action for the character. Ask children to create other dilemmas and possible responses which they swap with other pairs and discuss the results.

Activity Sheet 2

Suggest to the children that they imagine someone behaving badly, for example, bullying another child or taking something that doesn't belong to them. Encourage the children to discuss, in small groups, the dilemma that they face and what alternative courses of action are available to them. Provide them with the activity sheet and ask them to make notes for a story about the issue or dilemma using the first person voice. Encourage them to write a polished version of the story.

Activity Sheet 3

Cut out the dilemma cards from the activity sheet and place them face down on a table. Arrange the children into two groups. Choose children to pick up a card and read it aloud. Ask them then to walk down the conscience corridor. The children on one side say why the character should behave in one way and the other children say why they should behave in the opposite way. Finally, the child with the dilemma should choose which action to take and say why. Ask other children to pick other dilemma cards and repeat the activity. Encourage the children to choose one of the dilemmas and use it to write a short story using either the first or third person voice.

REFLECTION & FEEDBACK
suggestions

Ask the children to read their stories aloud for the other children during plenary sessions. Invite the children to say if having a dilemma or issue to write about helps them include a problem and resolution in their story writing. Ask children to review a story with an issue or dilemma, using the writing frame on Resource Sheet 37.

Getting Started

Book display

Encourage the children to create their own book display of stories that raise issues and dilemmas that they have enjoyed or think they might enjoy.

Ideas

Draw up a class list of issues and dilemmas that are relevant to the children's own lives to use as ideas for writing.

Same or different?

Read several short stories that raise issues and compare similarities and differences in the plots and how the characters deal with the issues.

However

As a group, tell a 'however' story. Begin with a sentence, for example, 'George wanted to play football.' The next person continues the story beginning with 'However...' Another child adds a third sentence and the fourth continues by adding another sentence beginning 'However…' and so on.

Hot seat

'Hot seat' children in the role of a character from one of the stories. Invite the other children to ask questions about how the character deals with an issue or resolves a dilemma.

What should he do?

Learning Objective: To explore two different courses of action in response to a dilemma.

Name _____ **Date** _____

With a partner, read the synopsis of the beginning of the story. Write what you think might happen to the character for the two choices he could make.

Jon was walking to school one morning when he saw an elderly lady drop her purse on the pavement. The woman didn't notice and carried on walking.

a) Jon runs and picks up the purse. He gives it back to the lady.

_____

_____

_____

_____

_____

_____

_____

_____

b) Jon looks around to see if anyone notices. He picks up the purse and puts it in his pocket.

_____

_____

_____

_____

_____

_____

_____

_____

What should I do?

Learning Objective: To plan a story about an issue or dilemma.

Name _____ Date _____

Make notes to plan a story about what happens when you see a younger child being bullied in the school playground. Use the prompts to help you organise your ideas.

The Bully

Beginning
In the playground: What did you see?

What did you think about doing?	What else did you think about doing?

What did you decide to do and why?

Middle
What happened next? A problem.

How did you solve the problem? Did anyone else help?

Ending
How does everyone feel now?

Activity Sheet 3
Conscience corridor

Learning Objective: To explore different ways to resolve dilemmas.

Name _____ **Date** _____

My Mum wants me to babysit my little sister, but I want to play out with my mates. What should I do?

A new kid has come to my class. He seems shy, a bit geeky but looks unhappy. Should I ask him to join my friends or just ignore him?

I found a really cool mobile phone. Should I keep it or hand it in?

My parents have told me not to play on the building site, but all my mates play there. Should I stay away from it or join my mates?

I have got some important homework but I really want to try-out for the first team after school. Should I do the homework or go to the try-out?

I woke up this morning and found I had turned into a girl! Should I tell someone about it or just ignore it and hope it'll go away?

DIALOGUE AND PLAYS

Purpose	to interest, entertain and amuse; sometimes also to inform and instruct
Structure	often sequential events; a clear beginning (introducing characters, setting & plot), middle (expanding on events and introducing the complication) and ending (resolution); sometimes includes flashbacks
Language features	usually past tense; mainly action verbs; descriptive language and dialogue; first and third person pronouns
Examples	*Playtime* (anthology) by Julia Donaldson; *Fantastic Mr Fox* (play) and *The BFG* (play) by Roald Dahl

Cross-curricular suggestions

Drama
★ Children put on a performance of a play for other children to watch. Talk about how the play might differ if they were performing it for Year 1 or for parents.

ICT
★ Children use video recorders to record role-play and performance.

Literacy
★ Children listen to a radio play and note the differences if a performance is heard and not seen. Then adapt a play they know, just for radio.

Teacher's notes

Use the **Challenge Cards** (Resource Sheet 45) to extend the unit.

Activity Sheet 1

Together read the play 'The Boy Who Cried Wolf' (Resource Sheets 39 – 41). Display an enlarged copy of the first two scenes (Resource Sheet 40). In a shared session, read and annotate the text. Provide the children with a copy of Resource Sheet 39 and ask them to annotate the following features: title, cast list, scene description, actors' names, stage directions. Then the children read the passage of dialogue on the activity sheet and rewrite it using the layout and conventions of a playscript. Before doing the activity, read the dialogue together and ask the children to suggest what is going on, how Danny feels and how Lee might be feeling. Encourage the children to try to convey their feelings through stage directions. Resource Sheet 42 can be used.

Activity Sheet 2

Display the annotated model text of dialogue, Resource Sheet 43 and remind the children about the conventions of layout, language and punctuation when writing dialogue. In this activity, the children read a playscript as a group. Encourage them to take notice of stage directions and to read with expression. Ask them to re-write the script on the activity sheet as a narrative dialogue, using speech verbs to convey the same expression as in the play and correct layout and punctuation.

Activity Sheet 3

In this activity, children demonstrate their understanding of the difference between playscript and narrative by writing the correct features into the correct place on the activity sheet.

REFLECTION & FEEDBACK suggestions

Discuss the difference between playscript dialogue and story dialogue. Invite them to try reading a script as if it were a story and vice versa. Ask the children to say why the two types of dialogue are written differently. How does each help the reader?

Punctuation

?:/"*,\"!-.

Give children a sentence of dialogue to say in turn, from Resource Sheet 44. Cut out the punctuation marks (also on the sheet) and ask the other children to hold up the appropriate punctuation for the sentences.

The example from *Bill's New Frock* in Stories with Familiar Settings (Resource Sheet 8) could be used. Enlarge a copy and mark up the punctuation, reporting clauses and paragraphing.

?:/"*,\"

Book display

Encourage the children to create their own book display of play scripts they have enjoyed or think they might enjoy.

Story or play?

Discuss what play scripts are and compare and contrast how dialogue is written in stories and play scripts. Ask children to find a play of a novel and with a partner note some of the differences.

Hidden plot

Watch films or DVDs of plays based on familiar stories. Discuss how the plot is conveyed through what the actors say and do. Talk about how this is different in narrative stories.

Act it out

In small groups, act out a familiar story, folk or fairy tale or short play they have found in the library.

Story dialogue into playscript

Learning Objective: To change a narrative dialogue into a playscript.

Name _____ **Date** _____

Read the paragraph of dialogue from a story and re-write it as a playscript in the writing frame below. The first part has been done to help you.

Best Friends

Danny ran up to Lee in the playground. "Lee," he panted, "found you at last. Is your dad taking you to the adventure park at the weekend?"

"Yeah, I think so," replied Lee. "Why?"

"Our car's broken down so I can't get there. Can I come with you?"

Lee paused before answering. "Not sure," he said. "I'll have to ask my Dad. We might have too many coming already." Lee quickly walked away, leaving Danny standing there.

"Humph…" muttered Danny to himself. "What's up with Lee? He is being odd to me nowadays."

Danny wandered back towards the school, suddenly feeling quite lonely.

Title:	**Best Friends**	
Cast:	Danny Lee	
Scene 1		
Danny (panting)	Lee, found…	

Playscript into story

Learning Objective: To rewrite the playscript as narrative dialogue using correct layout and punctuation.

Name _____ Date _____

Re-write the playscript as a dialogue using the correct layout and punctuation.

Scene 1 A busy playground. Hanif and Joe are on the right side of the playground. A group of boys are on the other side.

Hanif (*angrily*)	Who has moved my skateboard?	
Joe	Don't look at me! I haven't touched your skateboard.	
Hanif	Sorry Joe, I wasn't blaming you, but someone must have taken it.	
Joe (*sighing*)	Not again! Where did you leave it this time?	
Hanif (*scratching his head*)	Right there. It was leaning against the wall. Now it's gone.	
Joe	Let's go and ask the others.	(*they walk across the playground to a group of boys*)

Story dialogue or playscript?

Learning Objective: To demonstrate understanding of the difference between story dialogue and playscripts.

Name _____ **Date** _____

Read the words/phrases in the box at the foot of the page and decide which to write on the book cover and which to write on the stage.

Warning: Some will be for both!

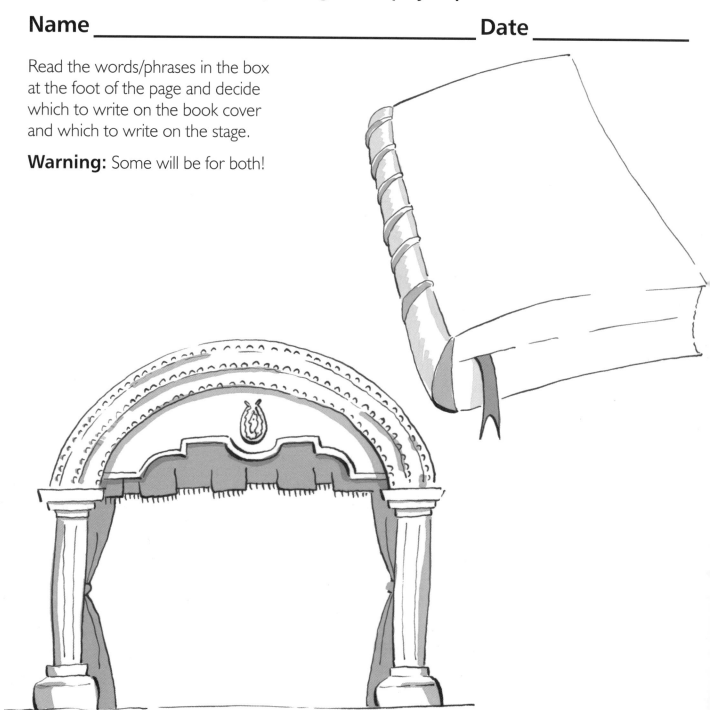

speech marks, cast list, reporting clauses (speech verbs with the speakers name)
new line for new speaker, paragraphs, stage directions, speech adverbs

LETTERS

Purpose	to recount events; to inform; to enquire; to complain
Structure	addresses; date; greeting; body of the letter; signing off
Language features	formal or informal language depending on the audience
Examples	*Letters to Anyone and Everyone* by Toon Tellegen; *Jamaica (Letters from Around the World)* by Alison Brownlie; *The Deathwood Letters* by Hazel Townson

Cross-curricular suggestions

History
★ Children research letters from the period in history they are studying. If possible make copies and display them for children to look at and compare with modern letters.

Literacy
★ Contact another school in your area and ask if you can correspond with them. Discuss how you will do that, for instance, the teachers might write letters to each other, but the children may prefer to send email messages. Compare the correspondence between the two schools.

PSHE
★ Children write a letter to invite a member of the fire service (or similar) to visit the classroom. After the visit, they write a letter of thanks.

Use the **Challenge Cards** (Resource Sheet 47) to extend the unit.

Teacher's notes

Activity Sheet 1

Display an enlarged copy of the model text on Resource Sheet 46. Discuss audiences of possible letters and draw up a list of possible letters for reference. Ensure the children are aware of the layout and language conventions of letter writing, and the use of formal and informal writing. If time permits, allow the children to discuss a selection of letters found in books and others which have been collected. The school office can often provide examples for discussion. Give the activity sheet to children in pairs and ask them to make notes for a response to the letter on the sheet. Then ask them to write a reply in their books.

Activity Sheet 2

In this activity, the children write two letters about a book they have read. One is to the author and the other is to a friend. They should make notes on the Activity sheet and use the prompts. When they have finished, display the letters and discuss the differences between them.

Activity Sheet 3

In this activity, the children are given a number of statements about an issue and use them to draft a letter of complaint using a formal tone and persuasive language. Prior to the activity, read one or two letters of complaint to the children and discuss the purposes, the level of formality and any persuasive language. Ask the children to suggest what the purpose of the letters is and whether they think the letters achieve the purpose. Give the activity to children in pairs and ask them to draft the main body of their letter on the sheet, using as many of the statements as they wish. Then ask them to write a finished copy of the letter in their books, including an address, formal greeting etc. If possible find an opportunity for the class to write a 'real' letter of complaint or concern to someone in the local community.

REFLECTION & FEEDBACK suggestions

Draw up a class list based on the children's ideas about when to be formal and polite and when to be informal and casual when writing letters.

GETTING STARTED

Letter writing

Provide the children with a selection of fiction and non-fiction books that feature letters. Encourage them to read the books to familiarise themselves with the conventions of letter writing.

Who's it for?

Collect and display a range of letters for different purposes and audiences. Invite the children to group them by formal or informal tone.

To and from

Choose a myth or legend and write letters between two of the characters. Encourage children to be 'in role' when they write the letters. Display the letters and the replies.

What's the point?

In a group or class session, discuss why we write letters to people. Draw up a list of purposes for letters and how their tone is affected by the audience and purpose.

Dear ...

Ask the children to work with a partner and to write a letter to each other informing them about a school event. Talk about how their letters were laid out and the vocabulary they used to set the tone.

Letter response

Learning Objective: To reply to a letter, using the correct layout and language conventions.

Name _____ **Date** _____

Read the letter and write a reply to it. Think about:

★ how to greet the person you are writing to

★ should you be formal, informal, or slightly informal?

★ how to sign off the letter.

Don't forget to put your address and the date on the letter.

The Skateboard Crew
Kingsbury Youth Centre
Brown Street
Longston
Lincs
L5 6YZ
2nd April 2010

Dear Faris

I am writing to invite you to attend the opening practice session of The Skateboard Crew. We are a group of young boys and girls who put on skateboarding displays at fairs, open days and other functions to entertain the public.

Our chief scout has seen you skateboarding and was impressed by your skill. We feel you could be a valuable member of the team.

I will be writing to your parents to make sure they are happy for you to take part in our exciting display team. In the meantime, please let me know if you are interested in joining us.

The practice session will be held at the Kingsbury Youth Centre on Friday 30th April at 6.30pm.

I look forward to your reply and hope to welcome you to the Crew.

Yours sincerely

Matt Foster

Matt Foster
Youth Activities Organiser
Kingsbury Youth Centre

Notes

Formal and informal letters

Learning Objective: To use formal and informal language to write about the same topic.

Name _____ **Date** _____

Choose a book you have read and enjoyed. 1) Write a letter to the author to tell them why you enjoyed it. 2) Write a letter to your best friend to suggest why they would enjoy reading it.

What do I want the letter reader to think/feel?

Dear or Hi?

Abbreviations?

Capital letters?

Yours sincerely?
Yours?
Love from?
Best wishes?

Exclamation marks?

Slang?

Complaining

Learning Objective: To write a formal letter of complaint using an appropriate tone and language.

Name _____ **Date** _____

You are writing a letter to the council to complain about the closure of the local swimming pool. Read the statements below about the issue first. Then draft your letter by organising and linking the statements in the most effective order.

★ There is only one swimming pool in the local area.
★ I believe this will be bad for everybody.
★ Many children use the pool after school and in the holidays.
★ Learning to swim is important.
★ It was announced in the local paper that the swimming pool is closing.
★ Many schools use the pool.
★ Children need exercise for a healthy life.

POETRY

Purpose	to entertain, puzzle, and appeal to emotions
Structure	various; sometimes written in stanzas, or shapes; font variations
Language features	may have rhyme, rhythm, imagery, onomatopoeia; words chosen carefully
Visual features	distinctive text layout according to form
Examples	narrative poems; shape poems; haiku; cinquain; limericks; performance poems; rap; sonnets

Cross-curricular suggestions

Drama
★ Children use drama techniques such as hot-seating, freeze frame and role-play to explore poetry.

ICT
★ Children use word-processing or presentation software to write their own poems and illustrate them.

Design
★ Design and make a poetry tree, on which children can 'post' their poems. Use a special event as a focus.

Teacher's notes

Use the **Challenge Cards** (Resource Sheet 48) to extend the unit.

Activity Sheet 1

In this activity, the children swap the initial sounds of a phrase to create another phrase with humorous effect. They then write six of their own spoonerisms.

Activity Sheet 2

Brainstorm a list of common similes that the children are familiar with, such as 'as dry as a bone', 'as fit as a fiddle', 'as black as coal' and so on. Many of these similes will sound fresher to the children than to adults. Read to the children some poems which feature similes. Invite the children to cut out the nouns and adjectives on the activity sheet and experiment with putting them together to create unusual similes. Discuss their results. Ask them to identify any similes that use alliteration. Which ones are the most imaginative or sound best? Encourage them to work with a partner and make up some of their own.

Activity Sheet 3

Spend some time looking at examples of poems that play with language and use imagery. Ensure the children have become familiar with examples of alliteration, simile and metaphor and other uses of word play. Display an enlarged copy of the activity sheet, 'Poetry play time'. Provide the children with several poems that they have already become familiar with and some post-it notes. Invite them to work with a partner and find any examples of language play in the poems. Ask them to write the name of the poem on a post-it note and stick it onto the chart in the appropriate page. Use the chart heading to make a class display chart showing all the poems the children enjoy.

Activity Sheet 4

Have a collection of nonsense verse available for children as they work on this activity. Spike Millilgan's work is very popular with children. Ask the children to recite poems to each other, with verve. It will be noisy, but they need to experience the sounds. Then ask them to collect the nonsense words, and words which rhyme with them. They can use these to help them create their own poem. Poems could be recorded at the end of the session.

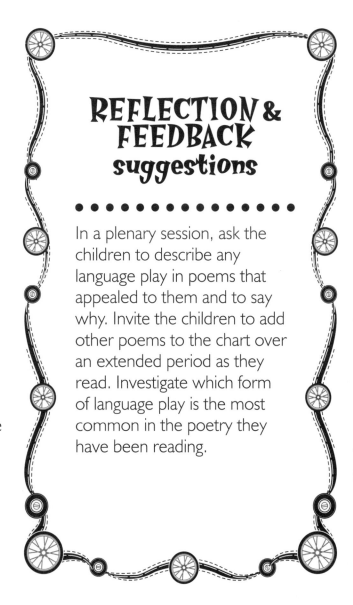

REFLECTION & FEEDBACK suggestions

In a plenary session, ask the children to describe any language play in poems that appealed to them and to say why. Invite the children to add other poems to the chart over an extended period as they read. Investigate which form of language play is the most common in the poetry they have been reading.

Book display

Provide a display of poetry anthologies of various styles and on various themes and encourage the children to read them.

Big book

Make a class big book collection of interesting, strange, amusing or exciting imagery from poems and display them on a wall.

Daily poem

Read a poem a day and encourage the children to join in with you.

Find the nonsense

Set children the task of sourcing nonsense verse; how many can they find? Explore why they are called 'nonsense'.

Poetry hour

Decide to have a poetry hour, once a month. Encourage the children to read aloud, with a partner, performance poems, poems with strong rhythms and rhyme and raps.

Riddles

At the end of each day, play games with words, such as spoonerisms, tongue twisters and riddles.

Spoonerism

Learning Objective: To explore poetry forms.

Name _____ **Date** _____

A spoonerism is a phrase where the initial sounds and or letters are swapped round. Sometimes more than one letter is swapped, for example, 'a crushing blow' becomes ' a blushing crow'.

Read the phrases on the left and rewrite them as spoonerisms on the right.

A pack of lies	
It's pouring with rain	
I hit my funny bone	
Jelly beans	
You've wasted two terms	
I'm lighting a fire	

Now invent six more spoonerisms.

Activity Sheet 2
Similes

Learning Objective: To play with words to create imaginative similes.

Name _____ Date _____

Cut out the nouns and adjectives at the bottom of the page. Experiment with arranging them as similes. When you have found the similes you think are best, glue them into place. Share them with a friend and together, make up some of your own.

As _____ as _____

As _____ as _____

As _____ as _____

As _____ as _____

As _____ as _____

As _____ as _____

adjectives	nouns
wet	frogs
terrible	hippos
jumpy	midnight
tall	demons
gloomy	ice-cream
hungry	boys
curly	lions
bouncy	wellies
cool	sunlight
dark	balloons
loud	coils
bright	jelly

Brilliant Ideas to Get Boys Writing 7–9 © A & C Black

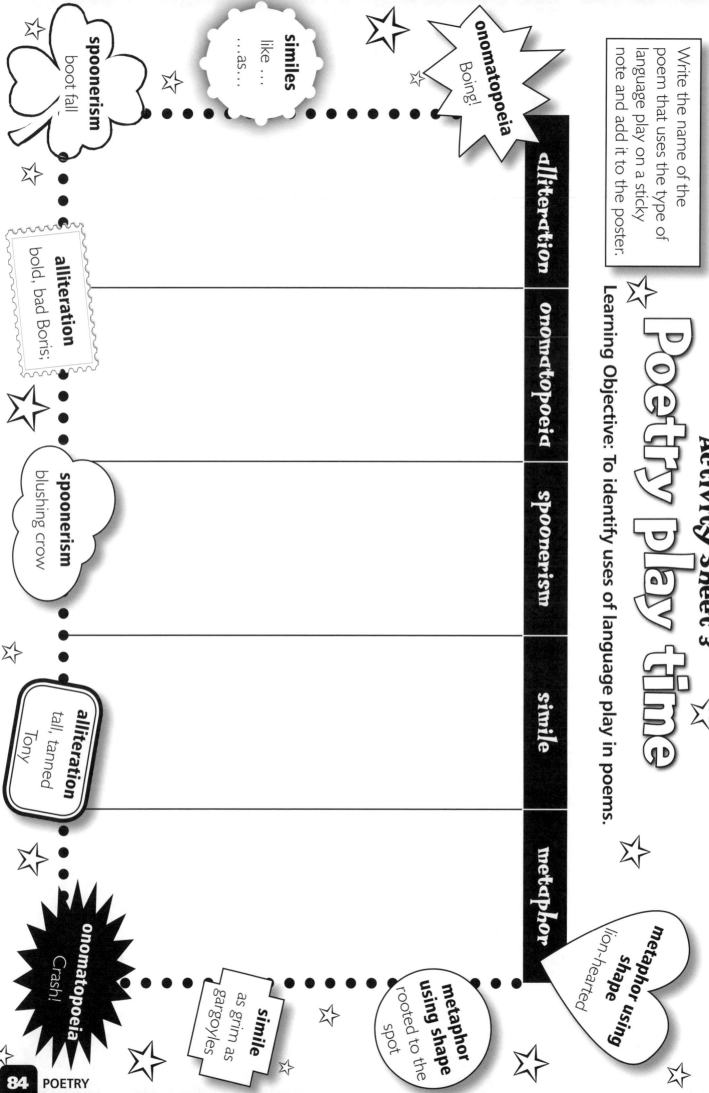

Activity Sheet 3

Poetry play time

Learning Objective: To identify uses of language play in poems.

Write the name of the poem that uses the type of language play on a sticky note and add it to the poster.

onomatopoeia
Boing!

similes
like …
…as…

spoonerism
boot fall

alliteration
bold, bad Boris;

spoonerism
blushing crow

alliteration
tall, tanned Tony

onomatopoeia
Crash!

simile
as grim as gargoyles

metaphor using shape
rooted to the spot

metaphor using shape
lion-hearted

alliteration	onomatopoeia	spoonerism	simile	metaphor

Lots of nonsense

Learning Objective: To identify uses of language play in poems.

Name _____ **Date** _____

Read the Edward Lear poem and compare it to the *Jabberwocky*. Make a list of nonsense words and words which rhyme with the nonsense words.

Ploffskin, Pluffskin, Pelican jee!
We think no birds as happy as we!
Plumpskin, Ploshskin, Pelican jill!
We think so then, and we think so still!
Edward Lear

nonsense words

rhyming words

Can you write a short nonsense poem? Recite it to your friend.

NON-FICTION

Most writing in the real world combines several text types. However, separating out the 'pure' text types and structures, explicitly naming their individual features can help students gain a better understanding. Explain and use these features and encourage boys to use them in their own writing.

★ Share books which appeal to boys and provide opportunities to respond to them – role-play, dramatisation etc.

★ Share books which appeal to boys and provide opportunities to respond to them, using a range of media, including electronic.

★ Create a bank of relevant vocabulary, phrases and prompts which help thinking, planning and reviewing.

★ Use *Talk for writing* principles and provide lots of opportunity to talk and collaborate prior to and throughout the writing process.

★ Display, demonstrate and discuss model texts and visuals and give a clear purpose for each task.

★ Ensure children discuss and agree text purpose and audience.

★ Provide questions for planning and a range of 'frames' for use.

★ Make available a range of tools, including ICT tools.

★ Display work in progress and finished work, in different versions.

★ Ensure opportunities for review and reflection are available and provide effective feedback.

REPORTS

Purpose	to present factual information, to inform the reader
Structure	introduction or general opening statement, followed by facts usually organised in paragraphs, with a conclusion or finishing statement; may contain an explanation sequence
Language features	present tense verbs; specialist vocabulary; third person, passive voice; comparisons and examples
Visual features	photographs, diagrams and illustrations
Examples	reference books; magazines; newspapers and electronic articles; alphabetically organised texts such as encyclopaedias

Cross-curricular suggestions

Geography
★ Children find the places in the world where wolves live using an atlas or globe.

Science
★ Children explore the life and habitat of the wolf.
★ Children explore adaptation of animal habitats.
★ Children look at endangered species and begin to explore the reasons for these.

ICT
★ Children use presentation software and computers to create reports about wolves.

Teacher's notes

Use the **Challenge Cards** (Resource Sheet 53) to extend the unit.

Activity Sheet 1

Arrange the children into groups and provide them with copies of the activity sheet. Give each group member one area of information which will become a paragraph in the report, i.e. the introduction, lorries, aeroplanes, trains, bicycles or the conclusion. Ask the children to read the sentences, cut them out and identify which ones belong to their specific area. They then arrange their sentences into a logical order. When everyone has ordered their sentences, ask the group to collaborate with reference to the 'Report Planning' (Resource Sheet 49) and stick them onto a larger sheet of paper to create a report about wheels.

Activity Sheet 2

Explain that when writing a report, first we have to research the topic. Find out and discuss what the children already know about wolves. Discuss ways of finding information, display 'Finding information'. In pairs, children discuss and complete the first three columns on the activity sheet. Encourage them to use books, the internet and other resources to research information to answer their questions and complete their chart.

Activity Sheet 3

Display Resource Sheet 50, hide the annotations and read the text together. Ask the children to identify the language and layout features which tell them this is report text. Provide the activity sheet and ask them to mark up the features of a report text.

Activity Sheet 4

Display again the 'Wild and Wonderful Wolves' (Resource Sheet 50). Ask the children to find the words written in bold print. Provide the children with copies of the activity sheet and dictionaries. Ask them to look up the words and write glossary entries for the report on wolves with a partner.

Activity Sheet 5

Provide the children with copies of the activity sheet and ask them to label the wolf diagram using the words in the text box.

Activity Sheet 6

Ask the children to refer to their charts from Activity 1. Explain that they are going to research and report on another class of wolf – the Red wolf. Ask them to work with a partner to find three facts about each of the areas on the activity sheet, including, if possible, at least one unusual or interesting fact. Allow the children time to research the topic using books and the internet. Display or provide Resource Sheet 51 and ask them to arrange the information into paragraphs before writing a polished version. Suggested websites; www.kids.nationalgeographic.com and www.enchantedlearning.com/subjects/mammals/dog/Redwolfprintout.shtml

Activity Sheet 7

Discuss all the different bears that children know or have heard about. Children work in small groups and write a report text titled 'Bears around the World'. Give groups a copy of the activity sheet and ask them to research the topic. Display Resource Sheet 52 to give them starting point ideas. Encourage the groups to talk together about what they have learned and make notes of titles, introductions, headings, important information and possible conclusions. Invite them to write a polished version of their report as individuals. Reports on different bears could be compiled into one book entitled 'Bears around the World'.

REFLECTION & FEEDBACK suggestions

During a plenary session, children describe what they have learnt about report writing. Invite them to describe how a writing frame or graphic organiser helps them to write report text. Invite them to evaluate the reports they have written and say which one they think is best and why.

GETTING STARTED

Share it

Use a shared reading session to draw up a list of the common features of report text, such as contents page, index, glossary, present tense verbs, headings and sub-headings, photographs, diagrams, paragraphs.

Explore a report

Ask the children to look at a report with a partner. Show the 'Text explorer' template on the whiteboard and ask children to review their report using these headings. Bring pairs into small groups to compare the reports they have been looking at. Make a chart showing the following from each report: Opening (what is the report about), Paragraphs (heading and main idea for each), Conclusion. Discuss their findings and display the reports and their findings.

News

Ask children to present a report of the week's news. Make sure the emphasis is on facts and not opinions.

Find the facts

Read a report to children (or have a group member read a report) and ask them to write down two or three important facts. Ask the group to discuss and put the facts in order of importance. Do all the groups agree?

Wolves on films

Watch both fiction and non-fiction films about wolves and compare their content and organisation. Suitable fiction could include *Peter and the Wolf*, *The Wolf and the Seven Little kids*. The National Geographic website has videos of Grey wolves on http://video. nationalgeographic.com/video/player/animals/ index.html
Hold a brainstorming session on 'What we know about wolves.'

Organising information

Learning Objective: To group related material into paragraphs.

Name _____ **Date** _____

Cut out the sentences about your specific area of information and arrange them into an order that makes sense.

WHEELS

Paragraphs:

introduction	No one knows when the wheel was invented or who invented it.
	These wheels run along a metal track.
	The number of wheels on a lorry depends on how big or heavy the lorry is.
lorries	The wheels that a plane uses to land on are large, but the wheel under the nose, used to move along the ground, is much smaller.
	Train wheels are different from lorry and bicycle wheels.
trains	Cycle wheels have many spokes between the tyre and the centre of the wheel.
	Aeroplanes have wheels as well as wings.
	Train wheels are made from steel.
aeroplanes	Cycles with three wheels are called tricycles.
	Wheels are used for many purposes.
	Lorries also have another wheel for steering.
bicycles	Some aeroplanes have two wheels but some have as many as 32.
	Unlike the wheels on lorries and bicycles, train wheels do not have tyres.
	Cycles with one wheel are called unicycles.
conclusion	Some large lorries have eighteen wheels.
	Although their basic shape remains the same (round), they come in many different sizes.

Wolf research chart

Learning Objective: To use a KWWL chart to research information.

Name _____ **Date** _____

Work with a partner to add notes to the chart showing what you already know about wolves. Add what you would like to know and where you might look for the information. Use books and the internet to find the information and then add it to the chart.

WOLVES	
What I **know** about wolves	
What I **want** to know	
Where can I look?	
What I **learned** about wolves	

Brilliant Ideas to Get Boys Writing 7–9 © A & C Black

Wild and wonderful wolves

Learning Objective: To identify the features of report text.

Name _____ Date _____

Mark up the layout and language features of this report on wolves.

Wild and wonderful wolves

Sub-species
There are several sub-species of the Grey wolf. These include the Great Plains wolf, the Indian wolf, the Mackenzie Valley wolf, the Mexican wolf and Tundra wolf.

The Great Plains wolf
It was thought that the Great Plains wolf had become **extinct** by 1926. However, later they were found in three states in the USA. They were given an 'endangered species' status in 1974 and since then their numbers have increased and are now classed as 'just threatened'.

Habitat
Great Plains wolves live in the western Great Lakes region of Minnesota, Wisconsin, Upper Michigan and Ontario. The size of the wolf's **territory** can vary depending on the type and availability of **prey**.

Appearance
Great Plains wolves vary from 137 cm to 198 cm long from nose to end of tail, and weigh between 27 kg and 50 kg.

Diet
The Great Plains wolf preys on white-tailed deer, moose, hares, small birds, and rodents.

Activity Sheet 4
Glossary

Learning Objective: To write a glossary for a report text.

Name _____ Date _____

Find out the meanings of the words in bold print in the 'Wild and wonderful wolves' report. Write a glossary entry for each word. Re-read the report and find any other terms you think should be in the glossary to help younger readers. Add them to the glossary. Remember to use alphabetical order.

GLOSSARY
carnivorous
conservationists
endangered species
extinct
mammals
Northern hemisphere
packs
prey
territory

Name _____

Date _____

Wolf appearance

Learning Objective: To label a diagram.

Use the words and phrases in the word box to add labels to the wolf diagram. Add any other labels you think are needed.

WORD BOX

black nose; keen sense of smell; large, sharp teeth, muzzle, strong jaws, thick fur, chest, shoulder, long legs, large paws, five toes, four toes, long thick tail, large pointed ears; keen sense of hearing.

The Red wolf

Learning Objective: To make notes for a report and use them to write a polished version.

Name _____ **Date** _____

Introduction

Habitat

Red Wolves

Appearance

Diet

Fascinating facts

Hunting

Bears around the world

Learning Objective: To collaborate with others to write notes for a report. To write a polished version independently.

Name _____ **Date** _____

With your group, make notes about different bears in the research grid and plan your report. Then write your own report about one of the bears.

BEARS AROUND THE WORLD			
Bear Introduction (Details)			
Appearance What they look like			
Habitat Where they live			
Diet What they eat			
Behaviour How they behave			
Conclusion Interesting fact(s)			

INSTRUCTIONS

Purpose	to describe how to do or make something or direct someone
Structure	heading to give goal or purpose; list of materials needed; sequence of steps in order; statement of outcome
Language features	action verbs – imperative; specialist vocabulary; present tense; time conjunctions to indicate order; adverbs
Visual features	bullet points or numbered steps; illustrations, photos and diagrams to support the text
Examples	recipes; directions; instruction and instructional manuals

Cross-curricular suggestions

Science
★ Children draw or write a set of instructions for a science experiment.

Art
★ Children instruct others clearly about the mixing of colours.

Design and technology
★ Children write a set of instructions for something made in Design and technology.

ICT
★ Children write instructions for using presentation software, such as how to insert a hyperlink. They can use a computer to write up instructions and add graphics.

Teacher's notes

Use the **Challenge Cards** (Resource Sheet 57) to extend the unit.

Activity Sheet 1

Discuss the different types of written instruction children are aware of. Display the chart on the activity sheet and discuss the column which has been completed, then ask children in pairs to complete the remaining columns. Ask them to find examples of each type of instruction text. Complete the class chart and make a display with examples. If time allows, ask each pair to look at and reflect on one example of an instruction text, using the 'text explorer' template on the CD.

Activity Sheet 2

Display Resource Sheet 54. Discuss the typical features of this type of 'How to …' instructional text. Look at the annotations and ask the children if there are other examples within the text. Ask the children to annotate the set of instructions on the activity sheet. Compare their annotations with the annotated text on Resource Sheet 55.

Activity Sheet 3

Provide the children with the activity sheet. Read the set of instructions aloud. Discuss what could be done to improve the instructions. Recap the features and layout that make a good set of instructions. Ask children to mark up words and sentences that need changing on the activity sheet and then re-write the set of instructions. If necessary some children can be provided with Resource Sheet 56 which can be cut up and the sentences re-ordered to create a clear set of instructions. Discuss the idea that sometimes numbers are added to instructions.

Activity Sheet 4

Provide the children with the activity sheet. Ask them to discuss with a partner the best adverbs that will help someone to understand how to perform the instructions on the page.

Activity Sheet 5

Provide pairs of children with copies of the activity sheet, if necessary photocopy to A3. Give one child a model car or a toy figure. Ask the other one to give them oral instructions about how to get from the 'starting point' to another place on the map, e.g. the library, the skateboard park, the playing fields and so on. Then change roles.

Activity Sheet 6

Give children the activity sheet and ask them to write their instructions as a set of directions to a specific point using the map on Activity Sheet 5. The task can be altered according to ability, with some children having a straightforward route and others having to travel via specific points. At the end of the activity ask children with the same instructions to share their work and note any differences in the directions. On the whiteboard use a flow chart to share two different routes to the same point.

Activity Sheet 7

Using a topic from another curriculum area that the children are familiar with, for example, design and technology, science or geography, use shared writing to explore how to write the instructions for an experiment or technique. Children can use the activity sheet to make their notes, then ask them to write their own polished set of instructions.

REFLECTION & FEEDBACK suggestions

Invite the children to follow the sets of instructions they have been working on to see if they work and how they could be improved. Draw up a list of the most important features needed for clarity.

GETTING STARTED

This is how...

Children bring in an object from home and give instructions so that another child can use it.

Barrier game

Children sit back to back in pairs. One child draws a simple picture or diagram. They then give their partner instructions to re-create the drawing. They then compare both pictures and work out what was needed to make the instructions easier to follow.

Make and do

Watch children's TV programmes that include 'make and do' features. Discuss the basic sequence of steps in the instructions.

Watch and instruct

One child performs a specific task, for example, making something or playing a game. The children observe and retell the actions as a list of instructions, so that someone else can replicate the procedure. Use a video recorder to check.

Commands

Discuss instructions that are seen around us, such as road signs. Explain what imperative or command verbs are and brainstorm a list of command verbs found on signs posts and road signs.

Make it clear

Pretend you are an alien who has absolutely no knowledge about something very ordinary, for example cleaning teeth. Bring in the necessary equipment – a toothbrush and some toothpaste. Ask the children to give you explicit instructions. Perform their instructions literally as they say them. For example, if they say 'put the toothpaste on the brush' you put the tube onto the brush, and so on. Then let the children do the same with a partner.

Activity Sheet 1
Instructions chart

Learning Objective: To identify the features of instructions texts.

Name _____ Date _____

Look at different texts which give instructions and add your ideas for the remaining columns.

	Instructions for a game	Craft instructions	Recipe	Directions
Purpose	To tell someone how to play			
Form	Sheet of paper Computer screen			
Headings	● Number of players ● How to play ● Rules			
Text	● Numbers for how to play ● Numbers for rules			
Illustration	Diagram with labels			
Audience	Children			
Example	Monopoly			

How to play marbles

Learning Objective: To identify the features of a set of instructions.

Name _____ **Date** _____

Mark the features of this set of instructions using coloured pens: Red – the purpose; Green – bullet point steps; Blue – command verbs; Yellow – list of what is needed; Orange – adverbs or adjectives; Brown – time based sequence words.

What you need:
One or more other children
A clear area of grass or soil
Several marbles each, including one large one for shooting

★ First find a suitable level area for playing the game.

★ Dig a small hole in the ground, about three inches deep.

★ Mark a circle around the hole approximately 1 metre in diameter.

★ To decide who goes first, flick a marble each towards the hole. The one with a marble nearest, but not in, the hole has the first turn.

★ Place all the other marbles randomly inside the circle.

The game
★ Flick your large marble towards the other marbles using your thumb.

★ If it propels another marble into the hole, pick it out and keep it.

★ If your marble misses, let someone else have a turn.

★ The winner is the person who has the most marbles at the end of the game.

Making a spider puppet

Learning Objective: To improve a set of instructions.

Name _____ Date _____

You will need

You should get a black glove, some buttons, a sewing needle and some thread to sew with.

What to do

First of all you should put the glove on and check where to put the buttons to make eyes. When you have decided that, make a mark. Sew the buttons on. Put the glove on and move it around like a spider. You can decorate it with wool or felt or other stuff.

Write your new instructions here.

Making a spider puppet

You will need

_____

_____

_____

_____

What to do

★ _____

_____

★ _____

_____

★ _____

_____

★ _____

_____

★ _____

_____

Activity Sheet 4
How should I do it?

Learning Objective: To choose appropriate adverbs to improve instructions.

Name _____ **Date** _____

Choose an adverb from the box at the bottom of the page for each instruction, to help someone understand how to do the action. Cut them out and try them in different sentences. When you have decided which adverbs fit the instructions best, stick them in the spaces.

[ ] fold the paper across the middle.

[ ] stir the mixture before it cools.

Hit it [ ] with a hammer.

[ ] dry before using.

[ ] add the liquid one drop at a time.

Put the fledgling [ ] back into the nest.

WORD BOX – ADVERBS

carefully	thoroughly
quickly	slowly
firmly	gently

Directions

Learning Objective: To give a clear set of oral instructions.

Name _____ Date _____

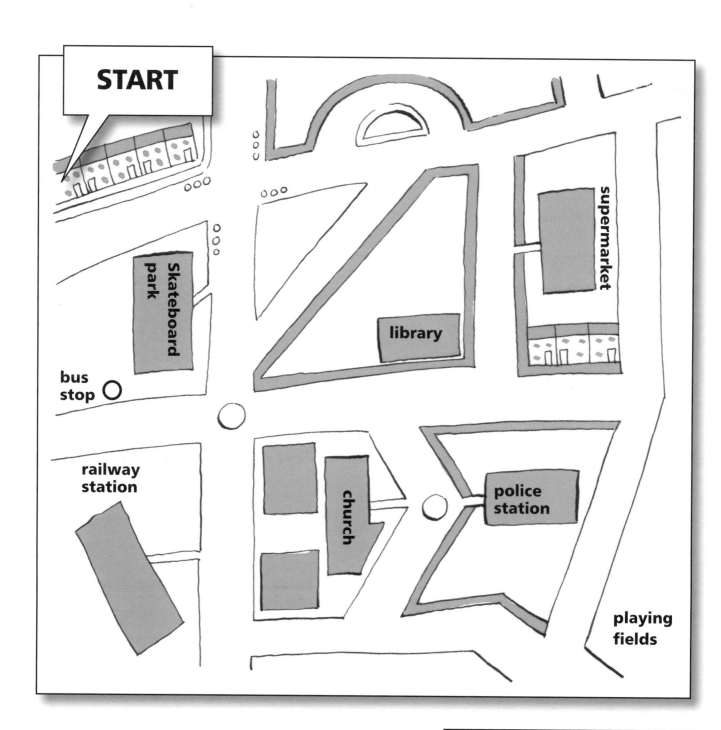

Tell your partner to put the car or figure on 'Start'.
Tell them how to get to a different place on the map.
Then swap roles.
How clearly can you give directions?
Did you use some of the words at the bottom of the page?

WORD BOX			
start	turn	left	right
keep	walking		until
when	you	reach	finally

Writing directions

Learning Objective: To write a set of directions with a clear layout and sequence of steps.

Name _____ **Date** _____

Use the map on Activity Sheet 5 to write the directions for your friend.

Directions from _____ to _____ .

1 Start at _____

2
_____
_____

3
_____
_____

4
_____
_____

5
_____
_____

6
_____
_____

Writing instructions

Learning Objective: To write a set of instructions with a clear layout and sequence of steps.

Name _____ **Date** _____

Write the title at the top	
What you need *(in order of use)* Do you need factual adjectives, e.g. colour, number, size and shape?	
Method *(Use a numbered list or bullet points for each step.)* Do you need time connective, e.g. first, next, later, finally? Do you need adverbs? Should you add a hazard warning or advice?	

RECOUNTS

Purpose	to describe an event or experience that has happened in the past
Structure	opening (orientation) sets the scene, followed by a sequence of events in chronological order and a closing statement
Language features	past tense verbs; first or third person voice; temporal or time connectives; evaluative or personal statements (opinions)
Visual features	photographs; illustrations; diagrams; maps and timelines
Examples	diary; letters; biography; autobiography

Cross-curricular suggestions

Geography
★ Children write a recount of a school trip which could include investigating places using visuals or a map and then draw their own map.

History
★ Having studied the life of a person in history, children write a recount for others to read.

Science
★ Recounts can be written after any growing or making experiments.

Design and technology
★ Recounts can be written to describe how items were created.

Teacher's notes

Prior to the activities, display Resource Sheet 58. Ask the children to read the text and to describe it (giving them information about a future event). Ask the children to say how it differs from a recount of an event. Change the text into a recount text together on the whiteboard. Give children a copy of the sheet to make their changes using their own words and past tense verbs.

Activity Sheet 1

Display Resource Sheet 59. Hide the annotations and read the text together. Invite the children to identify the language features that are typical of a diary recount. Reveal the annotations. Invite the children to annotate all the features on the activity sheet.

Activity Sheet 2

Ask the children to make notes in pairs, about a school event or trip using the activity sheet. Invite them to write their notes as a diary entry, individually or together.

Activity Sheet 3

Display Resource Sheet 60. Hide the annotations and read the text together. Ask the children to describe what type of text it is and identify the features that indicate this. Reveal the annotations. Ask the children to plan a recount of a school trip as a newspaper article using the prompts on the activity sheet, then write their newspaper article using the computer.

Activity Sheet 4

Display Resource Sheet 61. Hide the annotations and ask the children to read the text together. Invite them to say what type of text this is (letter) and its main purpose (to apologise and be allowed out of the shed). Explain that, as part of the apology, the letter recounts some events. Ask them to identify

recount features in the letter. Reveal the annotations. Invite the children to write a letter to a friend describing the school trip using the activity sheet and the notes they made on Activity Sheet 2.

Activity Sheet 5

Prior to the activity, review the children's time lines, if they made them (see Getting started). Display Resource Sheet 62 (obituary). Hide the annotations and ask the children to read the text and say what the text type and purpose is. Then encourage them to write a brief biography of a friend in the same style using the activity sheet.

REFLECTION & FEEDBACK suggestions

Invite the children to swap their recounts with a partner and discuss how they could be improved. Ask the children to say which type of recount they found easiest or most enjoyable to write and why.

GETTING STARTED

The news

Ask the children to watch or listen to a news broadcast on radio or television and to note down which items on the broadcast were recounts of events. The following day, ask them to describe one of the news items they identified as a recount and to say what features it contained that told them it was a recount.

Trip pictures

Make a pictorial sequence of an event such as sports day, or a school trip (or a mural in art). This helps children who find it hard to recall events.

Where and when

Ask the children, in small groups, to role-play a school trip, visit or other recent event to show the sequence in which everything occurred.

Temporal connectives

Brainstorm a list of temporal connectives and display as a class resource for the children to refer to during the course of working on recount texts.

Timeline

Ask children to make a timeline of their lives, adding important events to it. Display the timelines.

Recounts

Arrange a display of a variety of recount texts such as diaries, biography and autobiography, newspaper articles. Encourage the children to read the recounts and identify which type of recount they are – personal or factual.

Weekend words

Invite children to recount what they did at the weekend. During their oral recounts, write down words they use that are language features of recounts such as past tense verbs and temporal connectives.

Diary features

Learning Objective: To identify the features of diary writing.

Name _____ Date _____

Find and mark these features of a diary using different coloured pens: Green – past tense verbs; Blue – time words; Orange – opinions; Yellow – changes of print for effect; Red – setting the scene; Brown – closing statement; Purple – first person.

Wednesday April 1st

I played a brilliant April Fool's trick on my Dad last night. When he had gone to bed, I borrowed the keys to the shop. I sneaked out of the house and went to the sports shop. I wasn't sure what I was going to do at first, but when I saw the gleaming mountain bike in the front of the shop I had a brainwave. I took off its wheels and carried them home! I thought he'd be really puzzled where they had gone to. But when I hid them in the garden shed, I had an even better idea. So I sneaked back to the shop and took off ALL the wheels, not just bikes but everything!

I took all the wheels back to the shed. It took AGES. There were loads of wheels.

Eventually, at about 4 in the morning, I finished and went back to bed.

I can't wait to see his face! What a laugh!

Notes about an event

Learning Objective: To make notes showing who, what, when, where, how, why or feelings.

Make notes about the event using the writing frame. Add details about who was involved, what happened when, how you felt about it. Use your notes to write a diary entry about the event.

Who	What	When	Where	How/Why

Activity Sheet 3
The school trip

Learning Objective: To write a newspaper article.

Name _____ **Date** _____

Write a recount of the school trip for a newspaper article. Use the prompts to help you.
When you have finished, write it as a polished article on the computer.

Set the scene: Who? When? Where?	
What happened: Events in order; time words; details	
How did people feel about it: Opinions	
What did people say about it: Quotations	
Closing statement	

Letter to a friend

Learning Objective: To write an informal letter recounting an event.

Name _____ **Date** _____

Read your notes again from Activity Sheet 2 and improve them. Use them to plan a letter about the school trip to a friend. Write your finished letter on a separate piece of paper.

(address)

(date)

(greeting)

(write the events in order they happened)

(details, feelings and opinions)

(close the letter)

(sign off)

Activity Sheet 5
Biography

Learning Objective: To write a recount as a biography.

Name _____ Date _____

Ask your friend questions about himself using the headings on the page and make notes of their answers. Use the notes to write a short biography about their life so far. Remember to use the past tense (NOT the present tense) and to add details.

Name	
When born	
Where born	
Important events in life	
Favourite hobby: When it began	
Something most proud of	
Closing statement about the friend	

INFORMATION TEXTS

Purpose	to inform and classify information for readers
Structure	information grouped by topic area, sometimes in paragraphs; may or may not be written sequentially or in alphabetical order
Language features	generally present tense verbs, unless giving historical information; heading and sub-headings
Visual features	photographs; illustrations and various diagrams
Examples	most non-fiction texts including reports; instructions; persuasion; recounts; journalism and explanations

Cross-curricular suggestions

Art and design
★ Children design and illustrate an advertisement.

Science/Geography/History/Sport
★ Children create an information TV or radio programme about a topic.

ICT
★ Children use digital cameras and presentation software to make an information presentation or design a web page.

History
★ Children draw and label a family tree from the historical period they are studying.

Teacher's notes

Use the **Challenge Cards** (Resource Sheet 66) to extend the unit.

Activity Sheet 1

Children play a 'true or false' game in a group or with a partner. Provide them with a variety of information texts. Ask them to flick through the texts and find a fact. They then either say that fact aloud or make up a false fact. The other children have to guess if it is true or false. As a group, create a 'Fact and Fiction' book using the activity sheet. Each person writes either a genuine or false fact with a pop-up flap to show if it is true or false.

Activity Sheet 2

In this activity the children work with a partner to consider the statements on the activity sheet, and add two of their own. They decide if each statement is fact or opinion, cut them out and group them according to their decisions. They discuss their choices with another pair.

Activity Sheet 3

Ask the children to write down a few ideas about themselves on the activity sheet, in order to give a clear description to an alien from another planet that has no knowledge of children. Ask them to use the notes to describe themselves to the group. Encourage the others to listen carefully and say when they hear an opinion rather than a fact.

Activity Sheet 4

Provide the children with a printed web page from a social networking web site. Explain that they are going to write a web page for a friend. Allow children time to think of ten or so questions to ask their friend first. Invite them to talk to their friend and ask their questions. Then ask them to create the web page using the activity sheet. Tell them to add five or more facts about the friend and five or more opinions.

Activity Sheet 5

Discuss information programmes and documentaries that the children watch on TV. Ask them to suggest their own ideas for an information programme based on their own interests. Arrange them into pairs or small groups. Ask them to choose an idea and research information to use in their own documentary. They plan their programme using the activity sheet. Encourage the children to use digital cameras, presentation software, sounds and images to create their information programme.

Activity Sheet 6

Provide the children with some television listing magazines to explore and talk about any adverts for television programmes they have seen. Discuss the language that is used in promotional adverts for programmes. Ask the children to suggest words and phrases they could use to promote their own programmes. Ask them to design and illustrate a page for a TV listing magazine about their own information programme using the activity sheet. Children can use Resource Sheet 64 to help generate ideas.

Activity Sheet 7

Arrange the children into groups. Give each group a 'Topic facts' card from Resource Sheet 65. Alternatively the class can collaborate to write five or six facts about a recently covered curriculum topic. Place the 'Text type' cards from the sheet face down, so that pairs of children within each group can choose one. Explain that they are going to use the topic facts to write an information text using the text type they have chosen. They use Activity Sheet 7 to plan their information text, adding words and phrases and notes about the appropriate layout. Then each pair should create a polished version for display.

REFLECTION & FEEDBACK suggestions

Discuss and compare the different forms of information text the children have worked on. Ask them to say which they found most enjoyable and why. Play back and reflect on the children's programme presentations.

GETTING STARTED

Information texts

Provide a variety of information texts that present information in a variety of ways for the children to explore. Make a display of different diagrams and illustrations.

On the web

Print out a range of illustrated web pages. Ask the children to discuss the features of layout, illustration and design. Give each group one web page and ask them to locate all the information on the page. Discuss how this is different from information in book form and on film and television.

Fact or opinion

Give the children a familiar object each from the classroom, e.g. a pencil, a chair and so on. Ask the children to say aloud one piece of information about the chair. When a child gives a fact, they stand at one side of the room. When a child gives an opinion, they stand at the other side of the room. See how many children gave facts and how many gave their opinion.

What do you think?

Record some TV adverts and play them to the children. Pause the advert at several places and ask the children if the advert gave them a fact or an opinion.

Film makers

Record a documentary such as a wildlife programme or similar and show it to the children. Ask them to work in small groups or with a partner and role-play their own version of the same documentary. Encourage them to think up a new documentary and role-play it.

Fact or fiction

Learning Objective: To make a group true or false book.

Name _____ **Date** _____

Fold the page in half across the dotted line. Carefully cut around the flap. With the page folded, write a fact or something untrue across the page just above the flap. Lift the flap and write 'True' or 'False' in the space underneath the flap. Open the page and put a thin line of glue around the edge of the bottom half. Fold down again and glue it shut.

cut along the dotted line

fold here

glue along the edges

glue along the edges

glue along the edges

Activity Sheet 2
Fact or opinion

Learning Objective: To distinguish between fact and opinion.

Name _____ Date _____

Add two statements of your own. Which of the statements is a fact and which is an opinion? Discuss them with your partner and when you both agree, cut them out and put them into two groups on a sheet of paper.

Red is a colour.
Football is great!
Machines are tools.
Football is a sport.
Fizzy drinks come in bottles and cans.
Blue is my favourite colour.
The best way to score a goal is by heading the ball.
Tigers have beautifully striped coats.
Machines are useful.
The best cars can go very fast.
The fastest animal on land is the cheetah.
In a game of football, a goal is scored when the ball goes across the goal line.
Fizzy drinks are good for you.
Cars can be many different shapes and sizes.

Brilliant Ideas to Get Boys Writing 7–9 © A & C Black

Activity Sheet 3
All about me

Learning Objective: To give an oral description based on notes without giving opinions.

Name _____ **Date** _____

You have just met an alien who has never seen a child before. He wants to know all about you. Make some notes about yourself. We have provided some questions to start you off.

What do I look like?

What do I eat and drink?

What do I do?

Where do I go?

What do I wear?

All about us

Learning Objective: To write a web page that includes five facts and five opinions.

Name _____ **Date** _____

Design a web page for your friend. Include at least five facts and five opinions about them.

name		
Profile picture	**About me**	Hobbies
	What I am thinking	
Information		
Date of birth		
		Books
	Friends	
Gender		
Hometown		
		Movies
	Family	
Scared of		
Happiest when		

Information programme

Learning Objective: To research and write down ideas for an information programme.

Name _____ **Date** _____

Use the prompts to research and make notes for a television programme.

What is the programme about?	
Ideas for the title	Presenter(s)
Opening shot for the title	Introduction
Information for the middle scenes	How will I close the programme?
What do I want the viewers to think?	Am I giving my own or others' opinions about the subject?
Images and pictures for the programme	Closing titles
Sounds and music	

Activity Sheet 6
Advertise your programme

Learning Objective: To combine text and illustrations with persuasive language.

Name _____ **Date** _____

Write notes for an advert to promote your television programme.

Get attention! Explain how you are going to do this.	On a separate sheet, illustrate some of your ideas.
Say a little about the programme. Be brief and don't say too much or people won't need to watch it.	
Say when it will be shown.	
Say why it shouldn't be missed.	
End with a statement or a question that will stay in people's minds.	

Brilliant Ideas to Get Boys Writing 7–9 © A & C Black

Which type of text?

Learning Objective: To use language and layout appropriate to a specific text-type.

Name _____ **Date** _____

Plan your information text using these headings. Check the appropriate layout and language by looking at examples of the text type.

Topic: _____

Text type: _____

Purpose	
Audience	
Layout	
Headings (if needed)	
Important Words	
Appropriate language	
Illustrations	

explanations

Purpose	to describe how something works, or why something happens; explain a process
Structure	heading or initial statement signals of what is to be explained, followed by a sequence which describes 'how' or 'why', which can be time-based or based on cause and effect and sometimes a concluding statement
Language features	present tense verbs; subject-specific vocabulary; cause and effect connectives; time connectives; action verbs
Visual features	labels and diagrams including flow charts, cross-sections; photographs
Examples	scientific, technical and historical books, magazines and electronic articles; television and radio programmes

Cross-curricular suggestions

Design and technology
★ Children design an invention and explain how it works.

Science
★ Children explain the life cycle of a frog or other animal.

ICT
★ Children use presentation software to create a life cycle presentation.
★ Children paint or use collage to show a volcanic eruption. They use digital cameras to photograph each stage and create a moving image of an eruption using stop motion software.

Geography
★ Children research volcanoes around the world.

Use the **Challenge Cards** (Resource Sheet 70) to extend the unit.

Teacher's notes

Activity Sheet 1

Use a shared reading session to explore the features of explanation texts using Resource Sheet 67. Watch a video such as *Wallace and Grommit's Cracking Contraptions* on www.youtube.com. Other suitable examples are: *The Bully Proof Vest*, *Soccamatic*, *The Autochef* and *The Snowmatron*. Ask the children, in pairs, to make notes on the activity sheet to explain how the invention works. Encourage them to write their notes as a polished version.

Activity Sheet 2

Discuss cause and effect in everyday life: You forget your raincoat and it starts to rain – what happens? You are playing football and someone kicks the ball into the river – what happens? Give the children the activity sheet and ask them to work with a partner to add the effects and causes. If time permits, ask half the class to write some 'cause' cards and the other half to write some 'effect' cards. Swap the cards and see if they are able to furnish the appropriate cause or effect.

Activity Sheet 3

Invite the children to invent a 'Cracking Contraption' of their own. Brainstorm a few ideas with the children, such as a homework-writing robot, a dog walking machine and so on. Ask them to role-play using the contraption, then ask them to draw and label their invention and write how it works using the activity sheet.

REFLECTION & FEEDBACK suggestions

Invite the children to draw up their own list of the important elements of explanation text. In a plenary session, give them a simple set of instructions, such as how to make scrambled eggs, and ask them, orally, to change each step into an explanation.

Activity Sheet 4

Use a shared reading session to explore the features of the frog life cycle explanation and flow chart on Resource Sheet 68. Provide the children with copies of the activity sheet and ask them to add labels and captions to the flow chart to explain the process.

Activity Sheet 5

Use a discussion session to invent a new animal, bird or insect. Encourage the children to think of weird or monstrous crazy creatures. Talk about the creature's life cycle, does it lay eggs or have live baby versions of itself? Does it begin as one thing and then become something else, such as caterpillar/butterfly, dragonfly nymph/dragonfly? Ask the children to draw the life cycle of their invented creature with labels and captions to explain the life-cycle process. If time permits, ask them to write an explanation on the back of the sheet.

Activity Sheet 6

Explanations often use specialist vocabulary, so draw children's attention to glossaries in books and encourage them to search for specialist vocabulary and then to use dictionaries to locate the meanings of unknown words. In pairs, ask children to find the meanings of the volcanic words on the activity sheet which they will come across in the next activity. They can then locate words for other curriculum topics listed on the activity sheet. These lists can then be stored for future use.

Activity Sheet 7

Display Resource Sheet 69. Discuss the picture and ask them to describe what it shows, using the labels and captions to help them. Ask them to explain the process (sequence) orally. Provide them with the activity sheet and ask them to write an explanation text about how volcanoes erupt.

GETTING STARTED

Explain

In groups, give children topics and ask them to explain them to others in the group. Topics such as – Why we wear different clothes in summer and winter; How our bodies digest food; Why cyclist have to wear helmets.

Useful words

Encourage the children, in groups, to role-play natural phenomena such as a volcano explosion, flooding or a hurricane. They then compile a word bank of words they think would be useful for writing about natural phenomena.

☆ Wait ☆ a minute!

Record and then watch a children's TV magazine programme and pause it at strategic points. Ask the children if the item is recounting an event, giving instructions, reporting about a topic or explaining something. Ask them to identify words used that give them clues about the purpose.

What are you doing?

Ask one child to role-play a process from start to finish, for example, mending a puncture on a cycle tyre or milking a cow. Don't let the other children know in advance what the role-play is. Ask others to watch and say what is happening during the role-play. This could be done with a video camera, which will give children a chance to improve on their role-play before the class sees it.

How does it work?

Play an explanation game. Provide some simple everyday objects for the children. Ask a child to choose one and explain how it works. If the child uses an imperative (command) verb, their explanation has become an instruction so they have to pass the object to another child who explains how it works without using imperative verbs. When a child successfully completes the explanation, another object can be chosen. Suitable objects could include: a tin-opener, a screwdriver, a bicycle pump, a hairdryer, a stapler.

Cracking contraptions

Learning Objective: To make notes for an explanation.

Name _____ **Date** _____

Explain how the invention works. Make notes on the writing frame then write a polished version.

What is the name of the invention?

_____

What is the purpose of the invention?

_____

What happens first?

_____

Continue the sequence.

_____

What is the outcome?

_____

Things to think about!

★ Write how it works in the sequence of what is meant to happen.
★ Use the present tense.
★ Use some passive verbs such as, when the lever *is pulled*!
★ Use time connectives.
★ Use cause and effect sentences such as, this means that, when … it causes …!
★ If you are telling the readers how to work the machine themselves, you are writing *instructions*!

Cause and effect

Learning Objective: To understand the relationship between cause and effect.

Name _____ **Date** _____

Effect?

Look at these actions. What do you think the effect will be?

★ The boy pushed the light switch and
_____

★ There was no rain for a year which
_____

★ The river became blocked up so
_____

★ The polar ice is melting which
_____

★ The batteries were removed from the torch so
_____

★ Dinosaurs couldn't adapt so
_____

★ Goldilocks was hungry so
_____

Cause?

Look at these 'effects'. Can you add the 'causes'?

★ The head of the sunflower turned because
_____

★ Because _____
_____
the town flooded.

★ Our bodies are healthy because _____
_____

★ Because _____
_____ the paint
turned to green.

★ The sounds came out of the violin because
_____

★ Because _____
_____ the
boy fell over.

★ Arthur pulled the sword from the stone because _____
_____

My cracking contraption

Learning Objective: To draw and label an invention and explain how it works.

Name _____ **Date** _____

Draw and label your invention.
Explain how it works.

Name:

Purpose:

Sequence:

Outcome:

Which comes first – frogspawn or frogs?

Learning Objective: To add labels and captions to a flow chart.

Name _____ **Date** _____

Choose the beginning point on the flow chart. Write labels and captions to explain the process of development from frogspawn into frog.

Crazy creature life cycle

Learning Objective: To create a life cycle for an invented creature with labels and captions.

Name _____ **Date** _____

Draw the life cycle of your own crazy creature. Add captions and labels to explain how the creature changes from birth to fully grown.

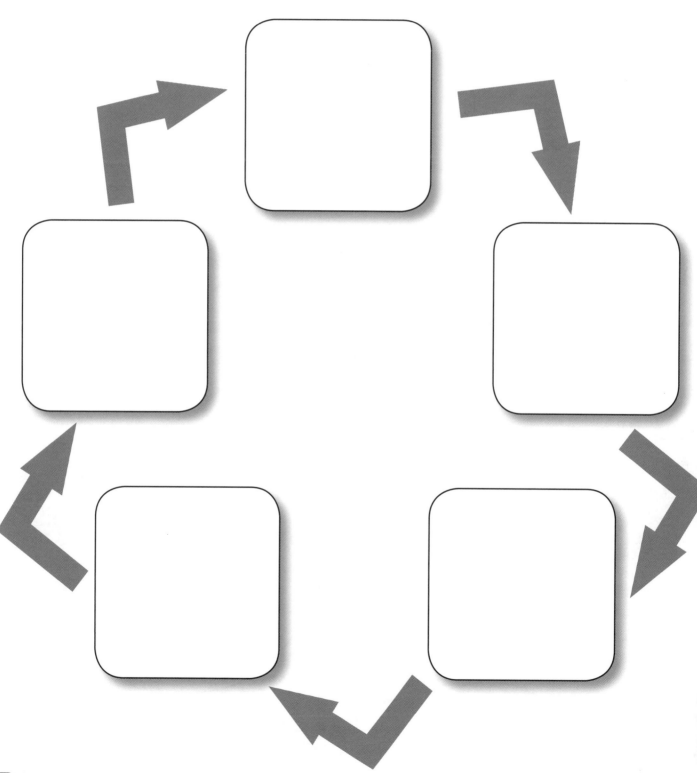

Specialist vocabulary

Learning Objective: To know how to locate and use specialist vocabulary.

Name _____ Date _____

Use a glossary to find the meanings of these words.

magma chamber

_____

central vent

_____

lateral vent

_____

crater

_____

lava

_____

Now find six specialist words for each of these topics. What do the words mean?

The water cycle

CAD design

An electrical circuit

How volcanoes erupt

Learning Objective: To write an explanation using present tense verbs and the language of cause and effect.

Name _____ Date _____

Write an explanation of how volcanoes erupt. Take care your explanation does not become a recount. Check that you have used present tense verbs.

	Introduction
	Eruption sequence
	Outcome

Write good time-connectives and cause and effect words to use.

PERSUASIVE TEXTS

Purpose	to persuade someone to act or think in a certain way or to argue a case for or against a point of view
Structure	positive statement followed by arguments in support and reinforcement; statement of point of view followed by arguments in logical order in support, elaboration and reinforcement
Language features	present tense verbs; emotive vocabulary; superlatives; time connectives; questions, instructions and commands
Visual features	illustrations and photos to support the text; use of different fonts and texts for effect
Examples	letters; advertisements; posters; leaflets; newspaper editorials; debates and speeches

Cross-curricular suggestions

Citizenship
★ Children explore letters to persuade for different purposes, audiences and situations.

PSHE
★ Children create posters to persuade others of the importance of exercise and healthy eating.

Science
★ Children explore the issues surrounding endangered species and make the 'for' and 'against' arguments for a particular course of action.

Teacher's notes

Use the **Challenge Cards** (Resource Sheet 72) to extend the unit.

Activity Sheet 1

Discuss the promotional posters, on Resource Sheet 71. Good alternatives are the free download of *The Incredible Hulk* poster or there are promotional posters for other films on: www.filmstreet.co.uk (search under poster). Ask children to say what the poster actually tells them about the film, and what it infers, e.g. how the colours, facial expressions and stills showing action from the film make them feel? What do they think the designer of the poster wanted them to think? Has it worked? Ask the children to write a paragraph to persuade someone to watch their favourite film or TV programme using the prompts on the activity sheet.

Activity Sheet 2

In this activity, the children (in pairs) have to persuade a friend who eats burgers and chips every day that eating a salad will be enjoyable. Explain that they should try to make the friend feel good about it, even excited, so they should use flattery and extravagant language. Use the activity sheet to make notes, but this could be executed as an oral or a written persuasion, or could be turned into a radio script or TV storyboard.

REFLECTION & FEEDBACK suggestions

• • • • • • • • • • • • • •

Discuss the persuasive techniques the children have used in the activities. Invite them to list them in order of effectiveness.

Activity Sheet 3

Suggest to the children that the idea for a burger-free day has been adopted by the whole class. Provide them with the activity sheet. Explain that they are going to design and create a poster to promote the idea. Ask them to cut out the phrases, arrange them to create an advertisement and illustrate it. They should add an attention grabbing heading and a sentence to close their advert. They can use the computer to create advertisements for display.

Activity Sheet 4

In this activity the children use the activity sheet to write a letter to you, their teacher, to persuade you to do activities outside on a sunny day instead of staying in the classroom.

Activity Sheet 5

Discuss an issue involving parents and school, for example, driving to school instead of walking, parking too close to the school, supporting the school football team more and so on. It might be useful to explore the issue through a drama activity before writing such as the 'Conscience Corridor' activity (Issues and Dilemmas Activity Sheet 3). Choose an issue and ask the children to use the activity sheet to write a leaflet to send to parents to try and influence their behaviour.

Activity Sheet 6

Discuss the idea of having more trees, in the playground or the local area. Tell children that they need to think about both positive (for) reasons and negative (against) reasons. Give the children Activity Sheet 6. Divide the class into two groups and give half the class the task of finding reasons for and half to find reasons against. At the end of ten minutes bring them together and write the reasons for both arguments on the board and discuss them.

Getting Started

Join us!

Ask the children to work in small groups. Each group should discuss 'what makes our group the best' then use their ideas to try to persuade one member of another group to leave their current group and join theirs.

After the children have had the opportunity to role-play persuasive situations, draw up a list of persuasive devices they have found worked well.

Why don't you?

Hold a discussion session about persuasion. Ask the children 'How do other people try to persuade you to do or think something?' Draw up a list of different occasions, such as letters, posters, different forms of advertising, both audio and visual.

Phone sales

Ask the children to try to persuade a partner to buy a new mobile phone that is full of amazing features. Ask the partner to say if it was successful or not and why.

Worth a visit

Give pairs of children a place to persuade others to visit – a museum, theme park or holiday destination. Children have to create either a poster or a short 'radio' ad to present to the class. Take votes on which venue children would most like to visit after the presentations.

Freeze frame

Discuss any films the children have enjoyed recently. In groups, children decide on an exciting moment from the film to freeze frame. They describe what is happening and try to persuade the other groups that they would like to see the film to find out what happens next.

Activity Sheet 1
Not to be missed!

Learning Objective: To write a paragraph to persuade someone to see a film.

Name _____ Date _____

Write a paragraph to persuade someone to watch your favourite film or TV programme. Tell them very briefly what it is about. Don't give away the ending! Use the prompts to help you.

Title of the film:

Introduce the film. What and who is it about? Say where it is set.

Three things that are special about it.

How will they feel while watching?

How will they feel after the ending?

How will they feel if they *do not see* the film?

Finish off by repeating one of your points. Try to use a different way of saying it. Can you write it as a question?

PERSUASIVE TEXTS
Brilliant Ideas to Get Boys Writing 7–9 © A & C Black

Activity Sheet 2
Try a Salad!

Learning Objective: To use the language of persuasion to change someone's attitude.

Name _____ **Date** _____

Persuade a friend that only eating burgers and chips is a bad thing. Encourage him to eat a salad instead. Use the prompts to help you.

Be positive! Get your friend on your side to start or he won't listen to the rest, so say something good about burgers such as 'Burgers are great aren't they, but did you know...

Still be positive! Flatter your friend but add a warning, such as 'You look great! So fit! But I know someone who...'

Tell him three things about how fabulous the salads taste.

Ask a question to make him think burgers are bad for him. He will then think it is his own idea! (sneaky!) For example, don't you want to be able to...?

Ask him to take action! Make him feel included and good about himself, for example, What are you waiting for? Let's grab a luscious salad before they are all taken!

Burger-free day!

Learning Objective: To select words and phrases to create an advertisement.

Name _____ **Date** _____

Choose the three phrases you think are the most effective to promote a burger-free day for the class. Cut them out and stick them onto a sheet of paper. Add an eye-catching heading and a final statement.

Salads are super!

Join us on healthy-eating day.

YOU WON'T MISS A BURGER.

Try it – you might like it.

Try Chilli for a Change!

TOO MANY BURGERS ARE BAD FOR YOU

WILL YOU TAKE THE CHALLENGE?

Have a burger-free day today!

Teacher! Teacher!

Learning Objective: To write a persuasive letter.

Name _____ **Date** _____

The forecast is for a sunny day tomorrow, after days of rain. Write a letter to your teacher to persuade him or her to let you do outdoor activities tomorrow instead of staying in the classroom.

Address:

Date:

Dear

Yours

Tips!

★ Begin by explaining the situation and what the purpose of the letter is.

★ Give three good reasons why being outside will be good for you and for the teacher. Flatter your teacher.

★ End with a positive statement about what you think your teacher will do.

Attention all parents!

Learning Objective: To write a persuasive leaflet.

Name _____ **Date** _____

Write a leaflet to influence the parents of children at your school. Continue the sentences and fill in the gaps.

★ Attention all parents! ★

The children of this school have noticed that ...

We believe that this ...

The reasons for this are ...

Also ...

Furthermore...

We would urge you to ...

Thank you

Should we plant more trees?

Learning Objective: To explore all the angles to persuade.

Name _____ **Date** _____

In the frame below, write your reasons for or against planting more trees.

SHOULD WE PLANT MORE TREES?	
Opinion (for or against)	
Reasons 1	
2	
3	
4	
Summary	

General reference sheets

These resources can be used as class discussion prompts, by children as part of activities or as classroom display.

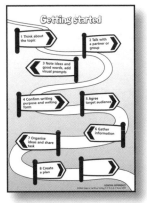

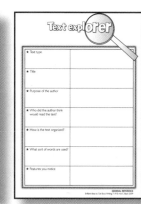

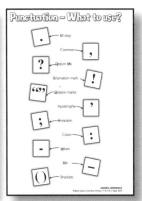

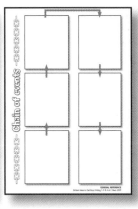

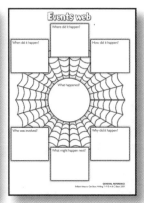

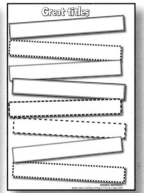